INSTANT POT COOKBOOK

Healthy, Easy & Delicious **VEGETARIAN** & **VEGAN** Recipes for Electric Pressure Cooker!

Box Set (2 in 1)

Table of Contents

INSTANT POT COOKBOOK

Healthy, Easy & Delicious VEGETARIAN Recipes for Electric Pressure Cooker!

Introduction

For the busy cook, your pressure cooker will seem heaven-sent. It enables you to make food that not only tastes great but that is easier to prepare as well. Throw in the fact that it cooks the food so much faster and it is clear we are on to a winner!

It is quite literally cooking using just one pot. You don't need to worry about having to do a bunch of dishes after slaving away at the stove anymore. The pressure cooker cuts out the need for a bunch of pots and shortens the amount of time that is spent in the kitchen.

I have included instructions for electric pressure cookers and also for a stovetop pressure cooker.

When it comes to vegetarian cooking, the pressure cooker is fantastic. Forget visions of peas boiled to within an inch of their lives – there is so much more that you can accomplish with a pressure cooker.

In this book, we are going to concentrate on vegetarian meals that are both extremely tasty and very nutritious as well.

You will have noticed that there are not too many recipes in this book that call for cheese. I do enjoy cheese but I know that not all people who follow a vegetarian lifestyle want to eat it so I have not used too much of it.

Cheese can always be added later if the mood strikes, so if you do eat cheese, feel free to experiment by adding it when you want to.

There is no longer any reason to grab a quick takeout on your way home from work. Cooking food in the pressure cooker is almost as fast and a whole lot healthier as well.

The recipes in this book are meant for two people, but most can be doubled: Cook double quantities and store one for a later meal.

Let's get started with pressure cooker meals that you will love!

Chapter 1: Breakfasts

Poached Free-Range Eggs and Tomato

Eggs and tomato are a classic breakfast combination. Make it nice and easy with this simple recipe.

Serves 2

5 big tomatoes

5 free-range eggs

3 level tablespoons melted farm butter

Seasoning according to taste

Put one and a half cups of plain water inside your pot. Slice the top off each tomato and remove the seeds inside.

Carefully crack an egg open and put into the hollowed-out tomato shell. Place the tomatoes into a heat-safe dish and place the dish into your cooker.

For Instant Pot: Using the manual setting, set to low pressure and cook for 5 minutes.

For Stove Top Cooker: Heat until low pressure is achieved. Cook for 5 minutes.

Sprinkle with pepper and the farm butter and serve with warm, wholegrain, farm buttered toast.

Beans and Eggs for Breakfast

This recipe is a little different in that white beans and tomato sauce are used in place of your normal baked beans. This gives a slightly different flavor and allows you to cut out the huge amounts of salt and sugar used in tinned beans.

Serves 2

5 free-range eggs, beaten

½ cup of full-fat milk

½ cup tomato-based sauce, home-made

2 whole garlic cloves, mashed

1 full cup white beans, pre-cooked

Seasoning according to taste

One teaspoon chili powder

Mix the eggs and milk together, beating well.

Mix in the other ingredients and pour into a heat-proof dish.

Put one full cup of plain water in your pot and place the dish inside.

For Instant Pot: Using the manual setting, set to low pressure and cook for 18 minutes.

For Stove Top Cooker: Heat until low pressure is achieved. Cook for 18 minutes.

Let off the pressure as you normally would.

Eggs Over-Cheesy

Is there such a thing as too much cheese where eggs are concerned? So far, I haven't found this to be true. Try for yourself with this recipe.

Serves 2

5 free-range eggs, well beaten

½ cup of double cream

1 level tablespoon of plain, full-fat cream cheese

½ cup of cheddar

½ cup of Swiss cheese

½ cup of mozzarella

Pepper to taste

2 whole garlic cloves, mashed

Beat together the eggs, cream and plain, full-fat cream cheese.

Add all the other ingredients and mix together.

Pour into a heat-proof dish.

Put a full cup of plain water in the pot. Put the previously prepared dish into your pot.

Close the lid.

For Instant Pot: Using the manual setting, set to low pressure and cook for 18 minutes.

For Stove Top Cooker: Heat until low pressure is achieved. Cook for 18 minutes.

Serve on toast.

South of the Border Breakfast

Serve this on tortillas with some freshly sliced chili pepper to really up the Mexican flavor.

Serves 2

5 free-range eggs, beaten

½ cup sour cream

½ cup fresh tomato salsa

1 onion, sliced into cubes

1 green pepper, sliced into cubes

1 full cup Pepper Jack

Mix together the eggs and cream and beat well.

Mix together everything else and pour into a heat-proof dish.

Add a full cup of plain water to your pot and add the dish.

Seal the pot.

For Instant Pot: Using the manual setting, set to low pressure and cook for 18 minutes.

For Stove Top Cooker: Heat until low pressure is achieved. Cook for 18 minutes.

Millet Porridge
Millet seems like a more old-fashioned grain but that doesn't make it any less delicious.

Serves 2

1 full cup of water

2 full cups of millet flakes

2 full cups double cream

One level tablespoon of coconut oil

3 level tablespoons of maple syrup

1 teaspoon of vanilla extract

1 teaspoon powered cinnamon

1 full cup almond farm butter

Dump everything into your pressure pot and mix well.

Seal the lid.

For Instant Pot: Using the manual setting, set to low pressure and cook for 2 minutes.

For Stove Top Cooker: Heat until low pressure is achieved. Cook for 2 minutes.

Let off the steam as you normally would.

Serve with your favorite toppings.

Oatmeal with Berries

Now granted, this is not something we normally associate with our pressure cookers but oatmeal can do well in the pressure cooker. Sometimes you need to tweak the water content a little so don't be too despondent if your first batch doesn't come out as well as you'd like.

Serves 2

3 full cups of water

2 full cups of quick-cook oats

2 full cups of assorted berries, frozen

2 level tablespoons of golden sugar

2 bananas, sliced into cubes

½ cup milk

Coconut flakes for garnishing

Nuts for garnishing, sliced into cubes

Mix together the oats and water in your pressure pot

Close the lid.

For Instant Pot: Using the manual setting, set to low pressure and cook for 6 minutes.

For Stove Top Cooker: Heat until low pressure is achieved. Cook for 6 minutes.

Then let it heat up till you get high pressure. Cook for 6 more minutes.

Let the steam out normally.

Garnish with whichever of the remaining ingredients you would prefer.

Chapter 2: Snacks

Refried Beans

For a quick protein burst, these are great. They are a great substitute for tinned beans.

Serves 2

4 ounces jalapeños, deseeded and sliced into cubes

1 level tablespoon of finely powdered chili

1½ cups of raw pinto beans

1 level tablespoon of cumin

¾ cup of homemade salsa

Salt to taste

Rinse your beans thoroughly and then allow them to strain. Put in your cooker. Submerge the beans in plain water and then add an extra two inches on top.

Seal the pot.

For Instant Pot: Using the manual setting, set to low pressure and cook for 45 minutes.

For Stove Top Cooker: Heat until low pressure is achieved. Cook for 45 minutes.

Let the steam out normally.

Put the beans back in the strainer to drain off the excess water. Transfer them to a bowl that is sealable. The beans should be completely cooked. Mix in the seasoning and blend until the beans are at the consistency you like.

Mix in the jalapeños and salsa and serve.

Superb Veggie Dip

Need something for game day that is not likely to cause a heart attack? This is not packed with as much fat and calories as most dips but still tastes awesome.

Serves 2

1 full cup mozzarella, finely shredded

10 ounces spinach, chopped coarsely

14 ounces tinned artichoke hearts, liquid discarded, coarsely chopped

1 full cup Parmesan, finely grated

½ cup sour cream

¼ teaspoon garlic salt

1 full cup low-fat mayonnaise

Cayenne pepper to taste

Mix everything well and place in a greased baking tin that will fit in your cooker.

Cover with heavy-duty foil.

Put in your pot, on a rack that will fit snugly into the pot. Pour a cup of water into the cooker.

Shut the pot.

For Instant Pot: Using the manual setting, set to high pressure and cook for 10 minutes.

For Stove Top Cooker: Heat until high pressure is achieved. Cook for 10 minutes.

Let the steam out as normal.

Be very careful when taking the pan out of the pot.

Pot Bread

This bread is great to have with breakfast or just on its own. It is also great for eating with soups and stews.

Serves 2

1.5 cups Greek yogurt

2 full cups of normal flour

One teaspoon of coconut oil

1 teaspoon of baking soda

Put a full cup of plain water into the pot.

Mix together the baking soda and flour and add the yoghurt.

Knead the resultant dough till it is completely integrated. Grease a heat-proof dish with the oil.

Put it inside your dish and sprinkle with plain water.

Completely close off using foil and put it into your pressure cooker.

Seal the pot.

For Instant Pot: Using the manual setting, set to high pressure and cook for 25 minutes.

For Stove Top Cooker: Heat until high pressure is achieved. Cook for 25 minutes.

Let the steam out normally. Remove the bread.

Serve warm with farm butter for breakfast or as comfort food.

Three Bean Chili

Again, if you want to increase your protein intake, this is a good place to start.

Serves 2

$^2/_3$ cup of raw, navy beans

$^2/_3$ cup of raw, black beans

$^2/_3$ cup of raw, pinto beans

1 red pepper, sliced into cubes

¼ cup of dried lentils

14.5 fluid ounces of canned tomatoes

2 level tablespoons finely powdered chili

6 ounces of tomato paste

1 level tablespoon powdered cumin

1 mild onion, sliced into cubes

3½ full cups of veg stock

2 celery ribs, sliced into cubes

2 whole pieces of garlic, mashed

Thinly sliced green onion (as garnish)

Put the stock into your cooker. Add your garlic, half the onion, the tomatoes, half the pepper, beans, lentil powder, cumin and chili.

Shut the lid.

For Instant Pot: Using the manual setting, set to high pressure and cook for 32 minutes.

For Stove Top Cooker: Heat until high pressure is achieved. Cook for 32 minutes.

Stir in the celery along with the rest of the vegetables. Heat your stove to a low heat and close the lid. Sauté for around ten minutes until the veggies are cooked through.

Caviar for Cowboys

Okay, so there are no fish eggs in this but it is still a really great dish. The flavors melt together and it tastes really special.

Serves 2

1½ cups of corn kernels

¾ cup of raw, black beans

1 full cup of raw tomatoes, sliced into cubes

2 level tablespoons of finely sliced cilantro

¼ cup of mild onion, sliced into cubes

½ cup of a red pepper, sliced into cubes

Sauce

Seasoning to taste

7¾ ounces of salsa

2 teaspoons of finely powdered chili

2 teaspoons of golden sugar

1 level tablespoon of rice vinegar

½ of a freshly-squeezed lime

Rinse your beans well and then strain them. Put in your pot and add 3 full cups of water.

Shut the lid.

For Instant Pot: Using the manual setting, set to high pressure and cook for 25 minutes.

For Stove Top Cooker: Heat until high pressure is achieved. Cook for 25 minutes.

Let off the steam as you normally would for ten minutes. Then let the beans strain.

Mix the sauce ingredients in a container that seals. **Note:** It must be big enough for the beans too.

Mix the rest of the ingredients together and coat well. Leave overnight so the flavors are able to really sink in.

Sloppy Joes

What would a recipe book be without Sloppy Joes in it? When you need to whip up a quick meal for yourself and your partner, this is simple and tastes great.

Servings 2

½ mild onion, sliced into cubes

½ cup of red, raw lentils

½ celery rib, sliced into cubes

2 ounces of tomato paste

¼ of a mild pepper, sliced into cubes

1 level tablespoon of golden sugar

2 level tablespoons of great quality red wine vinegar

1¼ cup of water

½ teaspoon of liquid smoke

2 whole pieces of garlic, mashed

Seasoning to taste

2 level tablespoonsful of breadcrumbs

2 hamburger buns

1 level tablespoon of your favorite hot sauce (optional)

If you like it hot, add the hot sauce. If you like it milder, leave the hot sauce out completely.

Reserve the breadcrumbs and stir everything else together in your pot.

Seal the pot.

For Instant Pot: Using the manual setting, set to high pressure and cook for 15 minutes.

For Stove Top Cooker: Heat until high pressure is achieved. Cook for 15 minutes.

Let the steam bleed off normally.

Take the lid off and stir the breadcrumbs through the mixture. Serve on the buns with some lettuce and tomato if you like. If you really like hot food, chop up some chili peppers, deseed and use as a garnish.

Vegan Hot Dogs

We used to love hot dogs when we were kids. That was before we understood how they were made. These make a passable vegetarian substitute – they wouldn't fool a hot-dog-eating champ but they are tasty and delicious.

Servings 2

Marinade

¼ cup of water

¼ cup of low-sodium soy sauce

1 level tablespoon of rice vinegar

½ teaspoon of finely powdered garlic

½ teaspoon of liquid smoke

½ teaspoon of powdered onion

The toppings that you want

For the "Dogs"

4 hot dog buns

4 big carrots, topped, tailed and scrubbed but not peeled

Place the carrots onto a metal rack that fits inside your pot and pour in a full cup and a half of plain water.

Seal the lid.

For Instant Pot: Using the manual setting, set to high pressure and cook for 3 minutes.

For Stove Top Cooker: Heat until high pressure is achieved. Cook for 3 minutes.

Let the steam bleed off quickly and check that the carrots are done. They are ready if they are fork tender.

In a sealable container or a zip-loc bag, mix together each of the ingredients in the marinade section. Add the carrots and marinade them in the refrigerator either overnight or for a whole day and night.

Just before you are ready to start eating, pour the marinade and carrots into your pot. Heat over a medium-high heat, uncovered, for ten minutes. Stir throughout the cooking time.

Use the carrots as you would normal wiener sausages and top with the marinade and your choice of toppings.

Chapter 3: Lunch

Ratatouille

Who doesn't love Ratatouille? The movie and the dish?
This is a classic version for those who love veggies.

Serves 2

1 potato, cut into small cubes

1 small eggplant, peeled and sliced into cubes

2 tomatoes, sliced into cubes

2 zucchini, sliced into cubes

¼ cup veg stock

4 level tablespoons top grade olive oil

2 green peppers, deseeded and julienned

2 whole pieces of garlic, mashed

2 level tablespoons of coarsely torn parsley

1 large onion, cut into small cubes

Put half the oil into your pot. Put the zucchini, eggplant, peppers and potato in.

For Instant Pot: Set your pot to "Sauté".

For Stove Top Cooker: Set your stove to medium.

Remove the veggies and fry the garlic and onion for a few minutes.

Put everything back into your pot and seal the lid.

For Instant Pot: Using the manual setting, set to high pressure and cook for 10 minutes.

For Stove Top Cooker: Heat until high pressure is achieved. Cook for 10 minutes.

Let off the steam fast.

Return the pot to your stove and let it simmer over a medium-high heat to thicken a little.

Potatoes with Beans

This again is enough for a main meal for two people. If you have leftovers, fry them up in some butter the next day for bubble and squeak.

Serves 2

3 potatoes, cut into small cubes

¾ pound green beans, sliced into cubes

1 green pepper, sliced into cubes

1 cup veg stock

1 onion, sliced into cubes

A whole clove of garlic, mashed

1 level tablespoon coarsely torn parsley

1 level tablespoon top grade olive oil

Put everything into your pot and mix.

Seal the lid.

For Instant Pot: Using the manual setting, set to high pressure and cook for 4 minutes.

For Stove Top Cooker: Heat until high pressure is achieved. Cook for 4 minutes.

Let the pressure release fast.

Kidney Beans from India

This is another alternative to plain, boring baked beans. Soak the beans the night before you plan to make this dish.

Serves 2

¼ onion, sliced into cubes

¼ pound of red, raw kidney beans

1 whole piece of garlic, mashed

1 tomato, sliced into cubes

½ thumb length of fresh ginger, cut up fine

1 teaspoon Greek yogurt

½ teaspoon garam masala powder

¼ teaspoon asafetida

¼ teaspoon turmeric powder

¼ teaspoon whole cumin seeds

¼ teaspoon powdered red chili

1 teaspoon coriander seeds, finely ground

1 teaspoon ghee or oil

1 sprigs coriander leaves, sliced into cubes

Salt to taste

1 cup plain water

Put the beans and water in your cooker and add salt and the turmeric.

Seal the lid.

For Instant Pot: Using the manual setting, set to high pressure and cook for 15 minutes.

For Stove Top Cooker: Heat until high pressure is achieved. Cook for 15 minutes.

While that is happening, fry the oil, cumin seeds and ginger on high heat for a minute or so. Put the onions in and fry them for another minute or so. Put the tomatoes in and cook for around five minutes.

Let off the steam normally.

Add the tomato mix to your cooker. Return your pot to the plate and let it simmer uncovered over a high heat for a few more minutes.

Add in the Greek yoghurt. Then bring it to the boil.

Garnish with the coriander.

Nutty Risotto

Risotto cooked the normal way is a bit of a chore. You need to attend to it almost constantly and, to be honest, for me it was too much bother. This way is so much easier that we now have risotto quite often.

Serves 2

1 full cup raw rice, Arborio is best

Seasoning to taste

2 level tablespoons of farm butter

$^1/_3$ cup walnuts

½ cup white wine, the drier the better

2 whole pieces of garlic, mashed

½ cup onion, sliced into cubes

¼ cup Parmesan, finely grated

3 full cups veg stock

Put the walnuts into your cooker and cook for a minute or so over a high heat, stirring all the time. Put to one side and chop them roughly when cool enough.

Put the butter in your pot. Then add in the chopped onions and the garlic. Fry for two minutes or so.

Add your rice and make sure it gets fully coated. Reserve the cheese and put all of the other ingredients into your pot.

Shut the lid.

For Instant Pot: Using the manual setting, set to high pressure and cook for 7 minutes.

For Stove Top Cooker: Heat until high pressure is achieved. Cook for 7 minutes.

Let the pressure drain off as normal.

Mix in the cheese and nuts and the risotto is ready.

Russet Potatoes Done Right

I know that potatoes have been getting a lot of bad press lately with all the low-carb diets doing the rounds. They are hard to beat when it comes to filling food that reminds you of your childhood, though. This is a very simple dish but tastes great.

Serves 2

Parsley, coarsely torn

1½ level tablespoon farm butter

1 whole piece of garlic, mashed

4 russet potatoes

Seasoning to taste

1½ cups of water

Find a rack that fits snugly into your pot and put it inside. Add the water and put the potatoes in as well.

Seal the lid.

For Instant Pot: Using the manual setting, set to high pressure and cook for 8 minutes.

For Stove Top Cooker: Heat until high pressure is achieved. Cook for 8 minutes.

Let the pressure release as normal.

Carefully take the potatoes out of your pot – they will be hot. Using an oven glove to protect your hand from the heat, slice the potatoes into wedges. Place in a serving bowl and top with the butter, garlic and parsley. Toss so that the potatoes are coated as soon as the butter melts.

Cheesy Risotto

This is just too delectable. The mozzarella melts to become nice and creamy and adds a lovely texture to this dish.

Serves 2

1 level tablespoon top grade olive oil

15 ounces tinned tomatoes, cut into cubes

1 full cup of onion, sliced into cubes

1½ cups of rice, Arborio is best

½ cup white wine, the drier the better

2 teaspoons Italian seasoning

½ cup green olives, sliced finely

2½ cups veg stock

1 full cup mozzarella, shredded finely

1 full cup parsley, coarsely torn

Seasoning to taste

Put the oil, seasoning and onion into the cooker.

For Instant Pot: Set your pot to "Sauté".

For Stove Top Cooker: Set your stove to medium.

Cook a few minutes over a high heat.

Mix in the wine and rice. Stir until the rice is coated. Reserve the parsley and cheese. Add everything else and seal the lid.

For Instant Pot: Using the manual setting, set to high pressure and cook for 5 minutes.

For Stove Top Cooker: Heat until high pressure is achieved. Cook for 5 minutes.

Let the pressure release fast.

Stir the cheese in and replace the lid. Let it sit off the heat just a little to let the cheese melt.

Serve with the parsley over the top as your garnish.

Spaghetti "Noodles" with Sauce

If you are somewhat tired of the same old pasta and sauce, this makes a nice change. Add in the extra vitamins and fiber you are getting and the classic Spaghetti with Noodles takes on a whole new healthy life.

Serves 2

1 full cup of water

1 spaghetti squash, halved down its width

2 full cups of a pre-prepared sauce of your choice – alfredo sauce, marinara sauce, etc.

Again, so simple that it should be against the law!

Put the squash onto a rack that fits snugly inside your pot and place it inside your pot. Add the water.

Seal the lid.

For Instant Pot: Using the manual setting, set to high pressure and cook for 20 minutes.

For Stove Top Cooker: Heat until high pressure is achieved. Cook for 20 minutes.

Let the pressure bleed off as normal.

Remove the squash carefully – it will be hot. Empty the pot of any remaining water.

Scrape out the squash flesh and put it back into the pot.

Pour in the pre-prepared sauce that you chose.

For Instant Pot: Set your pot to "Sauté".

For Stove Top Cooker: Set your stove to medium.

Cook until the sauce is warm all the way through. Stir all the time when doing this.

Peppers Stuffed with Veggies

Again, here the beans should be soaked overnight and rinsed off in the morning. You can cook them from scratch in your pressure cooker if you are willing to leave them in there for at least half an hour. This should help to remove any remaining substances in the beans that can cause gas.

For me though, it's just as easy to pop them in the pot overnight, covered with twice as much water. Either way they need to be rinsed so it isn't extra work to do it this way.

This recipe allows for two bell peppers per person. If that seems like too much for you and your partner, you can halve the ingredients. I find that this makes a nice main dish for two.

Serves 2

1 full cup Lima beans

4 mild bell peppers – lop their heads off and choose peppers that can stand relatively straight on their bases

2 level tablespoons finely powdered garlic

1 full cup quinoa – give it a quick rinse before using it

3 full cups veggie broth

1 full cup feta cheese

Reserve the peppers and the feta and put everything else into your pot. Stir very well and seal the lid.

For Instant Pot: Using the manual setting, set to high pressure and cook for 8 minutes.

For Stove Top Cooker: Heat until high pressure is achieved. Cook for 8 minutes.

Let the steam off quickly.

Stuff the peppers and top off with some of the feta.

Place under a broiler set on high for a little so that the peppers become heated right through and serve.

Carrot Noodles

This is another standby item for when you are tired of pasta. As mentioned before, I have never been a great fan of carrots but this recipe does disguise the flavor very nicely.

Using a spiralizer is the key to success with this recipe. Spiralize both the zucchini and the carrots.

Serves 2

2 full cups of zucchini

3 level tablespoons of top grade top grade olive oil

2 full cups of carrots

1 level tablespoon finely powdered garlic

2 full cups veg stock

3 whole garlic cloves, mashed

Seasoning to your liking

Simple as pie. Put it all into the pot.

Seal the lid.

For Instant Pot: Using the manual setting, set to high pressure and cook for 4 minutes.

For Stove Top Cooker: Heat until high pressure is achieved. Cook for 4 minutes.

Let the pressure release as normal and serve.

Parsnip Gratin

Serves 2

3 full cups of parsnip, finely cubed

3 level tablespoons of top grade olive oil

3 whole garlic cloves, mashed

Seasoning to taste

2 full cups of vegetable stock

1 level tablespoon finely powdered garlic

Two full cups Mozzarella, shredded

1 full cup of plain, full-fat plain, full-fat cream cheese

Reserve the mozzarella. Put everything else into your pot.

Seal the lid.

For Instant Pot: Using the manual setting, set to high pressure and cook for 4 minutes.

For Stove Top Cooker: Heat until high pressure is achieved. Cook for 4 minutes.

Let the pressure release as normal.

Serve with the mozzarella over the top of it.

Sweet Potato Bake
Serves 2

4 sweet potatoes, peeled and sliced wafer-thin

3 level tablespoons top grade top grade olive oil

3 whole garlic cloves, mashed

1 teaspoon finely powdered chili

2 full cups veg stock

2 full cups strong Cheddar, shredded

Seasoning to taste

One full cup plain, full-fat cream cheese

1 level tablespoon finely powdered garlic

Reserve the Cheddar. Put everything else into your pot.

Seal the lid.

For Instant Pot: Using the manual setting, set to high pressure and cook for 4 minutes.

For Stove Top Cooker: Heat until high pressure is achieved. Cook for 4 minutes.

Let the pressure release as normal and serve straight away.

Garnish with the Cheddar.

Quick Curry

This curry is so easy to make and tastes great. No one will believe it took about twenty minutes.

Serves 2

14.5 fluid ounces of tinned tomatoes, sliced into cubes

2 full cups of lentils – any kind of lentils that you like

13.5 fluid ounces of coconut milk

1 onion, sliced into cubes

3 level tablespoons of tomato paste

3 whole pieces of garlic, mashed

2 full cups of vegetable stock

3 full cups of water

2 level tablespoons of curry powder

1 full cup of spinach, sliced into cubes

1 teaspoon cayenne pepper

Fry the onion a little until it softens, add in the garlic bits and cook quickly.

Mix all of the other ingredients into the pot, except for the spinach.

Seal the pot.

For Instant Pot: Using the manual setting, set to high pressure and cook for 15 minutes.

For Stove Top Cooker: Heat until high pressure is achieved. Cook for 15 minutes.

Let the steam off normally, remove the lid and then stir through the spinach. Close lightly for a little while to let the spinach heat through completely before serving.

Lentil High Protein Stew
This is a great recipe for those cold winter days.

Serves 2

7 full cups of water

2 full cups of raw lentils

¼ cup of golden sugar

6 ounces of tomato paste

14.5 fluid ounces of canned tomatoes

1 level tablespoon finely powdered chili

1 teaspoon smoked paprika

1 full cup of corn kernels

1 red pepper, sliced into small cubes

2 teaspoons bouillon powder (optional)

1 teaspoon of cayenne pepper

2 tomatoes, cut into small cubes

2 celery ribs, sliced into cubes

Lightly rinse off the lentils. Let them drain a little, then put them into the pot. Stir in the tomatoes, tomato paste, sugar, water, spices and bouillon powder.

Shut the pot.

For Instant Pot: Using the manual setting, set to high pressure and cook for 15 minutes.

For Stove Top Cooker: Heat until high pressure is achieved. Cook for 15 minutes.

Let off the steam normally.

Put all the veggies in the pot. Sauté over a low heat, covered, for around 10 minutes until the veggies are cooked through.

One Pot Pasta

Again, pasta and high pressure cooking do not automatically seem to be a match made in heaven. They work together surprisingly well, though.

Serves 2

1 red pepper, sliced into cubes

½ a mild onion, sliced into cubes

3 whole pieces of garlic, mashed

1 pound of noodles

¼ cup of basil, fresh and Sliced into cubes

½ can of tomato paste

2 level tablespoons of sriracha sauce (if required)

3¾ cups of water

1 pound raw tomatoes, sliced into cubes

Fresh basil & black pepper to garnish

Put a quarter-cup of water into your cooker.

For Instant Pot: Set your pot to "Sauté".

For Stove Top Cooker: Set your stove to High.

Sauté the water, pepper, basil, onion and garlic for a few minutes, stirring continuously.

Stir in the tomato paste, noodles and water and mix well.

Close the lid.

For Instant Pot: Using the manual setting, set to high pressure and cook for 8 minutes.

For Stove Top Cooker: Heat until high pressure is achieved. Cook for 8 minutes.

If you prefer your pasta to be a little firmer, make it 6 minutes.

Let the pressure bleed off fast. Serve garnished, immediately.

Chapter 4: Dinner

Aloo Gobi

This can be described as spicy cauliflower and potatoes but it is so much more than that. It tastes fantastic and is extremely filling as well.

Serves 2

¾ pound of potatoes, peeled and cut into small cubes

½ whole cauliflower

½ average-sized, mild onion, finely sliced into cubes

Seasoning to taste

2 whole pieces of garlic, mashed

½ teaspoon of turmeric

1¾ full cups of water

½ teaspoon of coriander

1 teaspoon of garam masala

½ thumbnail of fresh ginger, mashed

½ teaspoon of red chili

Place the cauliflower onto a rack that fits into your pot and put it into the pot. Add ¾ cup of water to your pot and seal.

For Instant Pot: Using the manual setting, set to high pressure and cook for 2 minutes.

For Stove Top Cooker: Heat until high pressure is achieved. Cook for 2 minutes.

Let the steam bleed off fast and set the cauliflower aside to cool. Discard any remaining water.

Add a quarter-cup of cold water to your pot and put the garlic, ginger and onions into it.

For Instant Pot: Set your pot to "Sauté".

For Stove Top Cooker: Set your stove to medium.

Cook for about five minutes.

Add ¾ cup of water and stir. Put in the spices and potatoes and stir properly.

Seal the lid.

For Instant Pot: Using the manual setting, set to high pressure and cook for 8 minutes.

For Stove Top Cooker: Heat until high pressure is achieved. Cook for 8 minutes.

Let the pressure bleed off as normal.

While waiting for it to finish, ensure that you have cut the cauliflower into more manageable pieces. Stir it through the mixture in your pot.

Serve over the rice of your choice with some chutney on the side.

Carrot "Gravy"

I have never been someone who was in love with carrots. With this recipe, the taste of the carrots is understated and the overall effect is a recipe that is full of yummy flavors. I use this as a gravy over rice and mashed or roast potatoes.

Makes 2 full cups

½ a pound of potato, peeled & cut into small cubes

½ a pound of carrots, cut into small cubes

1 teaspoon of powdered onion

1 teaspoon of finely powdered garlic

2 full cups of water

2 level tablespoons of nutritional yeast

½ teaspoon of turmeric

Seasoning to taste

2 teaspoons of low-sodium soy sauce

Put the water in the pot and add the potatoes and carrots. The seasonings are not to be added yet.

Close the pot.

For Instant Pot: Using the manual setting, set to high pressure and cook for 7 minutes.

For Stove Top Cooker: Heat until high pressure is achieved. Cook for 7 minutes. Let the steam bleed off quickly.

Depending on the consistency that you want, you can either mash the carrots and potatoes and add the other ingredients or process everything in the food processor until smooth.

If you find that your gravy has turned out too thick, add some boiling water.

Black-Eyed Pea Chili

This chili is spicier than burning hot. If you want to increase the heat, use a very hot curry powder. Serve over rice, with poppadums or naan bread on the side. If you want to make it even hotter, make yourself some sambals to serve alongside it.

To make sambals, deseed and chop up a half a Jalapeno chili, half an onion and half a tomato. They should all be sliced into cubes. Serve on the side and use as a garnish.

Serves 2

2 full cups of water

¾ cup of raw black eyed peas

½ a teaspoon of ginger, grated

¾ cup of mild onion, finely sliced into cubes

3 whole pieces of garlic, mashed

7.5 ounces of tinned tomato sauce (NOT tinned tomatoes or tomato paste – tomato puree will work here as well)

½ teaspoon of mild or hot curry powder

Seasoning to taste

½ teaspoon of cumin

½ teaspoon of turmeric

1 teaspoon of garam masala

With the spices, try and locate a spice shop that mixes its own blends: they will be able to mix up whatever strength of curry powder or garam masala that you like.

As always, make sure that the peas are rinsed well and that there are no stones with them. Place the peas and the water into your pot.

Seal the lid.

For Instant Pot: Using the manual setting, set to high pressure and cook for 6 minutes.

For Stove Top Cooker: Heat until high pressure is achieved. Cook for 6 minutes.

Let the pressure release as normal and then strain off the water from the peas, reserving a quarter-cup of it. Set the peas to the side.

Add the reserved water to your pot and put in the onion, the garlic and the ginger. Cook over a high heat for five minutes. Stir often during this time.

Mix in the garam masala and turmeric and cook for a minute over high heat.

Add the curry powder, cumin, peas and tomato, stirring well to combine. Sauté for just a little longer until everything is heated through. Season if you think it needs it.

Quinoa Like You've Never Had It Before

Quinoa is one of those superfoods that have been used since ancient times and only recently come into focus in the health food world.

It makes an excellent substitute for rice and has one of the highest protein contents out of all the grains.

It has a somewhat nutty flavor and is easy to prepare – no wonder we love it.

Serves 2

2 full cups of red or white quinoa

2 whole pieces of garlic, mashed

2 full cups of water

1 level tablespoon of excellent quality rice vinegar

1 level tablespoon of low-sodium soy sauce

1 level tablespoon of granulated sugar

4 ounces of Asian veggies – use frozen if you need to, just make sure they are completely thawed when you are cooking them.

½ thumb-length of ginger, peeled and grated

Reserve the Asian veggies and put everything else into your pot.

Seal the lid.

For Instant Pot: Using the manual setting, set to high pressure and cook for 1 minute.

For Stove Top Cooker: Heat until high pressure is achieved. Cook for 1 minute. Let the steam release quickly.

Stir in the Asian vegetables and set aside covered in your pot again for a little while so that they warm through.

Gumbo

Who doesn't love a good old-fashioned gumbo? This one is hearty and extremely filling. Save any leftovers (like there'll be any!) and have them the next day. This does taste better the second day.

Serves 2

1 red, mild pepper, cut into small cubes

3 level tablespoons of excellent top grade olive oil

1 full cup of raw kidney beans, (soak them the night before you are making this meal and drain thoroughly)

3 whole garlic cloves, mashed finely

1 full cup cleaned mushrooms, sliced into cubes

2 zucchini, cut into small cubes

1 teaspoon powdered black pepper

2 full cups veg stock

2 level tablespoons of tamari sauce

This is such a simple recipe that it should be illegal. Put everything into your pot.

Seal the lid.

For Instant Pot: Using the manual setting, set to high pressure and cook for 8 minutes.

For Stove Top Cooker: Heat until high pressure is achieved. Cook for 8 minutes.

the pressure bleed off as your normally would.

You can serve with a nice Cheddar or Parmesan if you like.

Pasta Alfredo

This is one pasta dish that does not keep all that well. It doesn't go off quickly if kept in a sealed container in the refrigerator but the sauce gets soaked up into the pasta and it becomes dry.

This is one dish that you should never try freezing.

Serves 2

Sauce

½ full cup of water

1 whole cauliflower

4 whole pieces of garlic, mashed

1 full cup of spinach (it doesn't matter if you use fresh or frozen)

¼ full cup of nutritional yeast

½ full cup artichoke hearts (if you are using tinned hearts, drain all the liquid from them)

2 teaspoons salt

3 level tablespoons of fresh lemon juice

Pasta

3½ full cups of water

1 pound dry whole wheat fusilli pasta

Divide the cauliflower into quarters. Put it on a rack that fits well into your pot and add a full cup and a half of water.

Seal the pot.

For Instant Pot: Using the manual setting, set to high pressure and cook for 2 minutes.

For Stove Top Cooker: Heat until high pressure is achieved. Cook for 2 minutes.

Let the steam off quickly.

In your blender, mix together the spinach, the yeast, the hearts, the lemon juice, salt and garlic.

Blend in the cauliflower.

Clean your cooker and place the pasta in it. Pour over the sauce you just made and then add a full cup of water. Stir well. Repeat until all the water is finished.

The pasta should just be covered by the water.

Seal the lid.

For Instant Pot: Using the manual setting, set to high pressure and cook for 6 minutes.

For Stove Top Cooker: Heat until high pressure is achieved. Cook for 6 minutes.

Let the pressure bleed off fast and serve right away.

Vegetable Fiesta

If you enjoy your vegetables, you are going to go crazy for this recipe. It's almost like you are trying to cram all of your servings of veggies into one meal. There is enough here to use as a main meal for two people.

It really doesn't taste as good the next day so rather keep it as your main meal.

Serves 2

¼ pound Swiss chard, cut into small cubes

¼ pound Brussels sprouts, cleaned and halved

¼ whole cauliflower, sliced into cubes

¼ onion, sliced into cubes

¼ cup celery ribs, sliced into cubes

¼ zucchini, sliced into cubes

¼ cup of carrot, sliced into cubes

½ clove of garlic, mashed

¼ cup double Jersey cream

1 level tablespoon farm butter, melted

2 level tablespoons Parmesan, finely grated

1 full cup of water

Find yourself a microwave-safe bowl and mix in the cheese, cream, garlic and butter in it. Put to the side.

Put a rack that fits snugly into your pot into the pot and add the water.

Put the vegetables onto the rack.

Season to taste.

For Instant Pot: Using the manual setting, set to high pressure and cook for 7 minutes.

For Stove Top Cooker: Heat until high pressure is achieved. Cook for 7 minutes.

Let the pressure release fast.

When the vegetables are almost done, put the cream mixture into the microwave. Cook in one minute bursts on high, stirring between each, until the sauce is completely incorporated.

When the vegetables are done, drain them and serve with the sauce over them.

Toss to ensure that the vegetables are completely coated with the sauce.

Rice of Italy

This is ideal for serving with a hearty stew or casserole dish. Try it with a spicy veggie curry for something completely different.

Serves 2

¼ cup lemon juice

1½ level tablespoons plain, farm butter

3 full cups assorted, frozen vegetables (let them thaw before using)

1 sliced up mild onion

½ cup raw rice, use a wild grain or long-grained type

2 full cups veg stock

Seasoning to taste

2 teaspoons of powdered cumin

For Instant Pot: Set your pot to "Sauté".

For Stove Top Cooker: Set your stove to medium.

Put the butter into the pot and melt the butter. Add in the garlic and onion and fry until they soften a little.

Add in the rice and make sure it is all coated with the butter. Add each of the other ingredients.

For Instant Pot: Using the manual setting, set to high pressure and cook for 4 minutes.

For Stove Top Cooker: Heat until high pressure is achieved. Cook for 4 minutes.

Let the pressure release fast.

Fluff out the rice and serve it as is or as a base for another dish.

Grown-Up Brussel Sprouts
Serves 2

2 level tablespoons farm butter

1 pound Brussels sprouts, cleaned and halved

¼ cup of onion, sliced into cubes

¼ cup Parmesan, grated very finely

1 1/2 cups orange juice (if using frozen, let it defrost first)

1 level tablespoon low sodium soy sauce

Pepper to taste

2 whole pieces of garlic, mashed

For Instant Pot: Set your pot to "Sauté".

For Stove Top Cooker: Set your stove to medium.

Put the butter into your cooker. Add the garlic and onion and fry until they soften a little.

Reserve the Parmesan but add each of the other ingredients.

For Instant Pot: Using the manual setting, set to high pressure and cook for 5 minutes.

For Stove Top Cooker: Heat until high pressure is achieved. Cook for 5 minutes.

Let the pressure release fast.

Take the sprouts out and keep them warm in the meantime. Put your pot, uncovered, back on the stove and cook with a high heat. Add the cheese and mix together.

Add the sprouts. Warm until everything is piping hot.

Stewed Tomatoes Made Easy

I often use this as a substitute for tinned tomatoes. I will often double up the recipe and keep half to use in another recipe in the next day or two. If you do the same, this will keep for about three days if stored in a sealed container in the refrigerator. You can freeze the tomatoes as long as you plan to use them in a recipe later and not on their own.

Serves 2

1 level tablespoon top grade olive oil

4 very ripe tomatoes, skins removed

1 celery rib, sliced into small cubes

¼ green pepper, sliced into cubes

½ onion, sliced into cubes

1½ level tablespoons granular sugar

Seasoning to taste

½ teaspoon dried oregano

2 whole pieces of garlic, mashed

For Instant Pot: Set your pot to "Sauté".

For Stove Top Cooker: Set your stove to medium.

Put the oil into your cooker. Add the garlic, celery and onion and fry until they soften a little.

Add your tomatoes with their juice. Stir in a cup of water. Season to taste.

For Instant Pot: Using the manual setting, set to high pressure and cook for 5 minutes.

For Stove Top Cooker: Heat until high pressure is achieved. Cook for 5 minutes.

Let the pressure release fast.

Chapter 5: Side Dishes

Tropical Rice

Tropical rice is sweet, tastes rich and is very creamy. Use it as a breakfast dish or serve it as a dessert. It is also a great "salad" to take to a barbeque.

Serves 2

1¼ full cups of sweetened, half-fat or full-fat coconut milk plus 1/3 full cup

1 full cup of jasmine or basmati rice

1 full cup of frozen or fresh mango, sliced into cubes

Sesame seeds to garnish

2 level tablespoons of golden sugar

Take the rice and 1¼ cup of milk and put them into your cooker. You can use almond milk instead if you prefer.

Put the mango into your pot and seal it.

For Instant Pot: Using the manual setting, set to high pressure and cook for 4 minutes.

For Stove Top Cooker: Heat until high pressure is achieved. Cook for 4 minutes.

Let the steam bleed off normally.

Stir in the leftover milk until completely integrated. Serve straight away with the seeds and the sugar as your garnish

Black Bean Rice

If you are a vegetarian, there is a good chance that beans form an important part of your diet. They have oodles of protein and fiber and taste great – what's not to love?

These beans, paired with some brown rice, make for a complete meal that works every time. And, most importantly, if you use brown rice, it takes about the same cooking time that the beans do.

Serves 2

½ cup of raw black beans

1 full cup of brown or wholegrain rice

2½ full cups of water

½ mild pepper, sliced into cubes

½ mild onion, sliced into cubes

2 whole pieces of garlic, mashed

1 level tablespoon finely powdered chili

1 teaspoon powdered cumin

1 bouillon cube

½ teaspoon of cayenne pepper

For Instant Pot: Set your pot to "Sauté".

For Stove Top Cooker: Set your stove to medium.

Add about half a cup of water to your pot and put the garlic and onion in with it. Cook over a high heat for about five minutes.

Reserve the pepper and put everything else into your pot. Seal your pot.

For Instant Pot: Using the manual setting, set to high pressure and cook for 25 minutes.

For Stove Top Cooker: Heat until high pressure is achieved. Cook for 25 minutes.

Let the steam vent off as normal and then take off the lid.

Add the pepper just before serving.

Dahl

This traditionally accompanies curries and biriyanis and has a sort of sour and creamy flavor that is the perfect foil for the heat of the curry.

It is not to everyone's taste, so I advise serving it on the side and letting everyone choose how much they wish to use.

Alternatively, be a little different and use the dahl as a meal over rice just by itself.

Serves 2

6 full cups of water

2 full cups of raw lentils (green is more traditional but you can also use red if you like)

1 mild bell pepper, cut into small cubes

3 whole pieces of garlic, mashed

1 mild onion, sliced into cubes

The juice of ½ of a lemon

1 teaspoon of mild curry powder (stick to mild; the dahl should complement the flavor of the main meal, not compete with it)

1 teaspoon of turmeric

1 teaspoon of powdered cumin

¼ teaspoon of cayenne pepper

¼ teaspoon of fresh ginger, peeled and mashed

Put everything into your pot and stir very well.

Seal the lid.

For Instant Pot: Using the manual setting, set to high pressure and cook for 15 minutes.

For Stove Top Cooker: Heat until high pressure is achieved. Cook for 15 minutes.

Let the steam bleed off as normal and serve straight away.

Hummus

Hummus tastes great and is really good for you. The problem is that store-bought hummus is not always as healthy as we would like. Here you can make your own in a few minutes.

Serve it as a dip for plain crackers, chips or raw veggies.

Serves 2

2 full cups of water

1 full cup of raw garbanzo beans or chickpeas

2 whole pieces of garlic, mashed

The juice of ½ a lemon

1 teaspoon of powdered cumin

Seasoning to taste

Rinse the beans or chickpeas very well. If there are any loose dry husks, remove them. Set aside to drain for a bit.

Add water into the cooker and put in the beans/chickpeas.

Seal the lid.

For Instant Pot: Using the manual setting, set to high pressure and cook for 60 minutes.

For Stove Top Cooker: Heat until high pressure is achieved. Cook for 60 minutes.

Let the steam out quickly.

Put the beans/chickpeas into your food processor and add each of the other ingredients. Reserve some of the cooking water and add enough to make a smooth and creamy paste.

Mashed Potato

Okay so it isn't that hard to make mashed potatoes normally without a pressure cooker but I can assure you if you try these, you won't want to make them any other way again.

The potato comes out so light and fluffy and so soft that it melts in your mouth.

Serves 2

1½ full cups of water

1¼ pounds of potatoes, peeled and sliced into cubes

¼ teaspoon of onion powder

Seasoning to taste

¼ teaspoon of finely powdered garlic

½ teaspoon of Italian seasoning

Garnishes

¼ full cup of fresh green beans, topped, tailed and chopped

¼ full cup of fresh corn kernels

1 whole green onion, finely sliced

You'll notice that there is no milk listed for this mash. I find that it comes out just as nicely with water as it would with milk. Try it this way at least once. If you really want to, you can add some milk after the potatoes are cooked.

It's also important to maintain the same ratio of potatoes and water all the time. If you want to double up the recipe, that's fine as long as the ratio is maintained.

Lay the potatoes in your pot first and sprinkle all of the seasonings on top. You need to ensure that the potatoes come in contact with the seasoning at least once. Add in the plain water and stir if necessary.

Seal the lid.

For Instant Pot: Using the manual setting, set to high pressure and cook for 10 minutes.

For Stove Top Cooker: Heat until high pressure is achieved. Cook for 10 minutes.

Let the pressure release as normal.

Mash up the potatoes in your cooker and taste. If you feel you need to add a glug of milk, do so now.

Serve with the toppings and you are done.

Chapter 6: Sauces and Soups

Pumpkin Soup

Serves 2

3 full cups veg stock

3 full cups pumpkin, sliced into cubes

1 full cup full-fat coconut milk

3 whole pieces of garlic cloves, mashed

1 level tablespoons top grade olive oil

1 onion, sliced into cubes

Seasoning as required

One teaspoon powdered ginger

For Instant Pot: Set your pot to "Sauté".

For Stove Top Cooker: Set your stove to medium.

Put the oil, pumpkin, onion and garlic into your pot and cook for three or four minutes.

Put everything else into your pot.

Seal the lid.

For Instant Pot: Using the manual setting, set to high pressure and cook for 10 minutes.

For Stove Top Cooker: Heat until high pressure is achieved. Cook for 10 minutes.

Let the pressure release as normal and serve straight away.

Spud Soup
Serves 2

1 mild onion, cut into small cubes

3 full cups potatoes, sliced into cubes

3 full cups veg stock

2 whole garlic cloves, mashed

1 carrot, sliced into cubes

Pepper to taste

For Instant Pot: Set your pot to "Sauté".

For Stove Top Cooker: Set your stove to medium.

Put the oil, potatoes, onion and garlic into your pot and cook for three to four minutes.

Put everything else into your pot.

Seal the lid.

For Instant Pot: Using the manual setting, set to high pressure and cook for 10 minutes.

For Stove Top Cooker: Heat until high pressure is achieved. Cook for 10 minutes.

Let the pressure release as normal and serve straight away.

Vegetable Soup
Serves 2

1 mild onion, cut into small cubes

2 potatoes, sliced into cubes

2 whole garlic cloves, mashed

1 carrot, sliced into cubes

Pepper as required

3 full cups veg stock

1 full cup celeriac, sliced into cubes

½ full cup fennel, sliced into cubes

1 full cup ribs of celery, sliced into cubes

For Instant Pot: Set your pot to "Sauté".

For Stove Top Cooker: Set your stove to medium.

Put the oil, potatoes, onion and garlic into your pot and cook for three to four minutes.

Put everything else into your pot.

Seal the lid.

For Instant Pot: Using the manual setting, set to high pressure and cook for 8 minutes.

For Stove Top Cooker: Heat until high pressure is achieved. Cook for 8 minutes.

Let the pressure release as normal and serve straight away.

Broccoli Soup With "Cheese"

This is a really healthy version of this soup and contains no dairy at all. It tastes awesome and is really quite filling to boot.

Serves 2

½ a whole broccoli, cut into small cubes

1¼ pound of potatoes, peeled and sliced into cubes

1 carrot, sliced into cubes

Salt to taste

2 full cups of water

¼ teaspoon smoked paprika

½ teaspoon of finely powdered garlic

1 teaspoon chili powder

1 teaspoon of turmeric

1 teaspoon of lemon juice

⅓ cup of nutritional yeast

Put the broccoli onto a rack that fits well into your pot and put into the pot. Add half the water and seal the lid.

For Instant Pot: Using the manual setting, set to high pressure and cook for 3 minutes.

For Stove Top Cooker: Heat until high pressure is achieved. Cook for 3 minutes.

Let the steam release fast.

Take the broccoli out and chop it up. Drain any water from your pot and discard it.

Reserve the broccoli, lemon juice and yeast and add everything else into the pot.

Seal the pot.

For Instant Pot: Using the manual setting, set to high pressure and cook for 10 minutes.

For Stove Top Cooker: Heat until high pressure is achieved. Cook for 10 minutes.

Let the steam bleed off as normal.

Put the soup into your blender or your food processor and continue to blend till it is a thinner consistency. Add the remaining ingredients and blend well. Check the consistency of the soup. If you feel it is too thick, add boiling water.

Serve garnished with the broccoli.

Pea Soup

Soups were something that I used to avoid making before I had a pressure cooker. After all, who wants to sit around waiting for food that takes hours to cook? And then there is all the stirring, tasting, etc. involved. Cooking soup before was a schlep. Now it's a dream come true!

Serves 2

3 carrots, cut into small cubes

2 full cups of water

2 full cups of split peas

½ teaspoon of powdered black pepper

½ of a big, mild onion, sliced into cubes

2 full cups of veggie stock

2 whole pieces of garlic, mashed

Take about a quarter cup of water and put it into your pot. **For Instant Pot**: Set your pot to "Sauté".

For Stove Top Cooker: Set your stove to medium.

Add the garlic and onions and cook for about five minutes. Stir often so that the mixture doesn't stick.

Reserve the pepper and put everything else into your pot.

Seal the lid.

For Instant Pot: Using the manual setting, set to high pressure and cook for 7 minutes.

For Stove Top Cooker: Heat until high pressure is achieved. Cook for 7 minutes.

Release the steam as normal and let the soup cool a little.

Blend until it is the texture that you want. I find that leaving some of the peas whole does add a nice element when it comes to serving.

If the soup seems a little too thick, stir in some boiling water. The soup will only thicken more as it gets colder.

Black Bean Soup

This soup is packed with flavor and is extremely good for you. It is the perfect soup for when you need some serious comfort food.

Serves 2

1 big, mild onion, sliced into cubes

3 full cups raw black beans, thoroughly rinsed

1 carrot, sliced into cubes

6 whole pieces of garlic, mashed

2½ cups of water

3 celery ribs, sliced into cubes

1 level tablespoon of cumin

2 full cups of veg stock

¼ full cup of fresh, coarsely torn cilantro

1 teaspoon of finely powdered chili

The juice of a lime

1 teaspoon of cayenne pepper

A word of caution when using raw beans. Do make sure that there are not any pebbles in amongst them. These can easily slip in during harvesting and can be indistinguishable from the beans when cooked: and biting down on a stone is not a pleasant experience.

Keep back the cilantro and lime juice and put everything else into your pot. Stir well.

Seal the pot.

For Instant Pot: Using the manual setting, set to high pressure and cook for 55 minutes.

For Stove Top Cooker: Heat until high pressure is achieved. Cook for 55 minutes.

Let the steam bleed off as normal.

Blend the soup along with the cilantro and lime juice.

Serve with tortillas, salsa and avocados.

Marinara Sauce
Serves 2

1 can of tomato paste

1 pound of tomatoes, sliced into cubes

1½ cups of plain water

½ red pepper, sliced into cubes

½ mild onion, sliced into cubes

Seasoning to taste

1 level tablespoon of dried Italian seasoning

1 level tablespoon of golden sugar

¼ cup fresh, coarsely torn basil

3 whole pieces of garlic, mashed

Put about half a cup of water into your pot and add in your onion and your garlic.

For Instant Pot: Set your pot to "Sauté".

For Stove Top Cooker: Set your stove to medium.

Fry for around 5 minutes.

Reserve the basil and stir each of the other ingredients.

Seal the lid.

For Instant Pot: Using the manual setting, set to high pressure and cook for 15 minutes.

For Stove Top Cooker: Heat until high pressure is achieved. Cook for 15 minutes.

Let the steam bleed off quickly. Take off the lid. Then add in your basil. Blend until smooth.

For Instant Pot: Set your pot to "Sauté".

For Stove Top Cooker: Set your stove to medium.

Place back onto your stove and cook until it comes to a boil. Stir constantly and cook it for 10 minutes or so until nice and thick.

Lentil Soup

This soup is a meal in itself. The lentils are a great source of both protein and fiber, helping you feel full and stay full for longer.

Serves 2

1 mild onion, sliced into cubes

5 potatoes, cut into small cubes

1 full cup of green, raw lentils

2 carrots, sliced into cubes

2 celery ribs, sliced into cubes

2 bay leaves

15.5 fluid ounces of tinned tomatoes, sliced into cubes

1 full cup of green peas: frozen is better but use tinned if you have no choice

1 full cup of kale or spinach, sliced into small cubes – this can either be fresh or frozen, whatever is easiest

3 whole pieces of garlic, mashed

3½ full cups of water

2 full cups of veggie stock

2 teaspoons of black pepper

Reserve the kale/ spinach and the peas.

Put every ingredient into your pot and seal the lid.

For Instant Pot: Using the manual setting, set to high pressure and cook for 10 minutes.

For Stove Top Cooker: Heat until high pressure is achieved. Cook for 10 minutes.

Let the steam bleed off normally and take the lid off.

Mix in the spinach/ kale and the peas.

Put back on the stove on a low heat to allow the peas to heat through completely.

Take the bay leaves out and serve.

Hot Sauce

Yes, I realize that it is easy to find hot sauce at the store and that it isn't that expensive to buy. But have you seen what goes into some of the commercial brands of hot sauce? Making your own allows you to ditch all the chemical additives. It also means that you can make the sauce as hot as you want to.

Technically this is not a pressure cooker recipe. I cheat and use my pressure cooker on the Sauté setting. If your pressure cooker is manual rather than electric, you can use it as a pot to cook this sauce. Just leave off the lid.

Makes 2 full cups

3 level tablespoons of golden sugar

1 pound of hot jalapenos or Fresno chili peppers

6 garlic cloves, peeled

½ cup of high quality, distilled vinegar

Salt to taste

3/4 cup of water

You can use green chili peppers if you like as well: the only difference is that the sauce will be green in color.

Remove the stems of the chilies and blend them until fine. Add in everything else and blend until you have a liquid. If necessary, add some more plain water.

For Instant Pot: Set your pot to "Sauté".

For Stove Top Cooker: Set your stove to medium.

Cook the sauce for about 15 minutes. Stir often throughout the cooking time.

The sauce will last a couple of weeks if kept in a sealed container in your refrigerator. I advise against using plastic containers as the sauce can stain them. Use an old glass jar instead.

Corn Chowder

Serves 4

I have made this a double-up recipe. Keep half for some other time.

1 pound corn kernels

2 pounds of potatoes, peeled and cut up into small cubes

3 whole pieces of garlic, mashed

1 mild onion, sliced into cubes

1 red pepper, sliced into cubes

2 teaspoons smoked paprika

13.5 fluid ounces of full-fat coconut milk

2 full cups of vegetable stock

Green onion and cilantro finely sliced into cubes as a garnish

Seasoning according to taste

Put the garlic and onion into your cooker. Add around a quarter full cup of stock.

For Instant Pot: Set your pot to "Sauté".

For Stove Top Cooker: Set your stove to medium.

Sauté it all together for about five minutes. Mix the other spices and ingredients.

Shut the lid.

For Instant Pot: Using the manual setting, set to high pressure and cook for 8 minutes.

For Stove Top Cooker: Heat until high pressure is achieved. Cook for 8 minutes.

Let off the steam normally.

Blend half of the soup and then mix back with the rest of it.

Garnish it to taste and serve.

Potato and Carrot Soup

This is a good old-fashioned soup – something like your gran may have made for you when you were sick. It is a nutritious and filling soup and well worth adding to your repertoire.

Serves 2

8 carrots, cut into small cubes after peeling

5 medium potatoes, sliced into cubes after peeling

½ of a mild onion, sliced into cubes after peeling

3 whole pieces of garlic, mashed

¼ cup peanut farm butter, powdered

2 full cups of kale, finely sliced into cubes (Use fresh or frozen – whatever you have)

1 teaspoon of cayenne pepper

1 level tablespoon of mild curry powder

2 full cups of veggie stock

2 full cups of plain water

Take about a quarter full cup of the water and put into your pot.

For Instant Pot: Set your pot to "Sauté".

For Stove Top Cooker: Set your stove to medium.

Add in your onion and your garlic and fry, stirring quite often, for around five minutes.

Add the curry powder, peanut farm butter powder and cayenne pepper. Mix well so that a paste is formed, you can some more water if you need to. Fry this for two minutes over a high heat, stirring quite often.

Pop in everything except the kale and seal the lid.

For Instant Pot: Using the manual setting, set to high pressure and cook for 8 minutes.

For Stove Top Cooker: Heat until high pressure is achieved. Cook for 8 minutes.

Let off the steam normally.

Blend the soup until it is the consistency that you want. Add the kale and blend again.

Conclusion

Well, that's all for now. Thank you once again for taking the time to read this book.

I hope that I have inspired you to change the way that you look at your pressure cooker. I hope that you have been inspired to dust it off and put it back into use.

Enjoy yourself and have fun with the recipes. Once you have gotten the basics down when it comes to pressure cooking, there is a world of new tastes that await you.

I encourage you to start using your pressure cooker – take the drudge out of cooking and save time to do what you really want to.

Have fun with it!

Finally, I would like to ask one small favor of you. Would you mind leaving a review of this book on Amazon for me? I would truly appreciate it.

VEGAN INSTANT POT COOKBOOK

Healthy, Easy & Delicious VEGAN Recipes

for

Electric Pressure Cooker!

Copyright 2017 by Maria Hopkins

the trademark owner. All trademarks and brands within this book are for clarifying purposes only and are the owned by the owners themselves, not affiliated with this document.

Introduction

Thank you for checking out my new book, "Vegan Instant Pot Cookbook".

Choosing to become a vegan can be extremely fulfilling from a spiritual standpoint but it can be tough when it comes to creating food that is delicious.

In America today, we place a lot of reliance on processed foods, meat and cheese and so switching to a simpler way of eating can be a tough sell.

You do not have to miss out on flavorful meals that are quick and easy to prepare, though.

Pressure cooking allows you to prepare food that is bursting with flavor in so much less time than normal cooking.

The recipes listed here have been designed not only to be easy when it comes to preparation, but also really delicious, allowing you to eat good, wholesome food.

I have, as normal, given the instructions for both an Instant Pot and for a stovetop cooker for each recipe. If you have an electronic cooker other than the Instant Pot, I urge you to read through your cooker's manual. You might need to make one or two small adjustments.

The recipes that are here are meant for two people. I have also included recipes that are bulkier so that you can cook ahead and freeze the leftovers.

Enjoy your new book and let's get cooking!

Chapter 1: Breakfasts

Plain Millet

Serves 2 to 3

1¼ cups of distilled water

¾ cup millet

Fine salt

If you are using an electronic cooker or an Instant Pot: Set it to "Sauté".
If you have a manual cooker: Heat your stove plate to a medium-high heat.

Put the millet in your pot so that it toasts nicely. Be sure to stir it at all times. Once it starts popping and smelling toasty, you can add the water.

Close your pot's lid.

If you are using an electronic cooker or an Instant Pot: Put it on the manual setting and choose a high pressure. Set the time for 10 minutes and allow the pressure to be naturally released.

If you have a manual cooker: Heat your stove plate to a medium-high heat and allow the pressure to build up until it is high. Then cook for 10 minutes. Let the pressure release naturally.

Take the lid off with care in case there is any steam left.

Have a look at the millet. If you can see any white bits, it is not properly cooked and you need to cook it for a few more minutes.

Let it rest for two to three minutes and then fluff out. Add salt if need be.

Lemon-Flavored Millet
Serves 2

1 garlic clove, skins removed and crushed

½ cup leek or onion chopped up nice and fine

½ cup millet, thoroughly rinsed

1½ cups home-made veggie stock or distilled water

1 cupof veggie greens of your choice, chopped into bite-sized pieces

½ tablespoon zested lemon/ lime rind

Fine salt

1½ tablespoons of lemon or lime juice

If you are using an electronic cooker or an Instant Pot: Set it to "Sauté".

If you have a manual cooker: Heat your stove plate to a medium-high heat.

Put the millet in your pot so that it toasts nicely. Be sure to stir it at all times. Once it starts popping and smelling toasty, you can add the leek/ onion and garlic. Fry fast for around a minute.

Add the stock.

Close your pot's lid.

If you are using an electronic cooker or an Instant Pot: Put it on the manual setting and choose a high pressure. Set the time for 10 minutes and allow the pressure to be naturally released.

If you have a manual cooker: Heat your stove plate to a medium-high heat and allow the pressure to build up until it is high. Then cook for 10 minutes. Let the pressure release naturally.

Take the lid off with care in case there is any steam left.

The greens go into your pot next. Place the cover over them and letthem wilt in the residual heat in the pot for a few minutes.

Take off your lid and add the zest and juice. Add salt if need be.

Wheat Berry, Barley, and Nut Salad
Serves 2

⅓ cup of wheat berries

½ cup of pearl barley

1⅓cups of distilled water

1½ tablespoons of organically-sourced olive oil

2 tablespoons of lemon or lime juice

½ teaspoon fine salt

1 celery rib, sliced up nice and fine

2 big garlic cloves, skins removed and crushed

Pepper if you want to add it

½ scrubbed carrot, sliced up nice and fine

2 tablespoons of toasted nuts, either almonds or hazelnuts that have been crushed

¼ cup parsley, flat-leafed or Italian, sliced up coarsely

Put the berries, distilled water and barley inside the cooker.

Close your pot's lid.

If you are using an electronic cooker or an Instant Pot: Put it on the manual setting and choose a high pressure. Set the time for 25 minutes and allow the pressure to be naturally released.

If you have a manual cooker: Heat your stove plate to a medium-high heat and allow the pressure to build up until it is high. Then cook for 25 minutes. Let the pressure release naturally.

Take the lid off with care in case there is any steam left.

Place the grains into a big serving dish and leave for about 20 minutes so that they can cool off.

In a smaller bowl, you need to mix the seasoning, the oil, the garlic cloves (skins removed and crushed,) and the lemon/lime juice.

Mix the grains with the nuts, carrot, celery rib, parsley(sliced up coarsely) and the dressing. Set aside for at least 15 minutes.

Alternatively serve chilled.

Quick Traditional Steel-Cut Oats
Serves2

Pinch of fine salt

½ cup almond or soya milk, distilled water, or fruit juice

1 cup of distilled water

½ cup traditional steel-cut oats

Put the water into your cooker along with the milk/ fruit juice. Add the salt together with the oats but do not stir them in.

Close your pot's lid.

If you are using an electronic cooker or an Instant Pot: Put it on the manual setting and choose a high pressure. Set the time for 3 minutes and allow the pressure to be naturally released.

If you have a manual cooker: Heat your stove plate to a medium-high heat and allow the pressure to build up until it is high. Then cook for 3 minutes. Let the pressure release naturally.

Take the lid off with care in case there is any steam left.

Stir now and check the texture of the oats. If they are still too watery, put the lid back on and set aside.Let it rest for just a few minutes.

The oats can be eaten straight away. Alternatively, you can make a big batch – it will last for 3-4 days if refrigerated and will last for about a month if frozen on the day it is made.

Flavoring the Oats

To change up the flavor, add a stick of cinnamon, some cardamom seeds or a star anise before you start cooking. (Discard the cinnamon or star anise when serving.)

You can substitute whatever spices you like. I enjoy mine with a sprinkling of nutmeg just before serving.

You can also use dried fruit to make things more interesting. Just add a half cupful of whatever dried fruit you like before you start to cook.

Alternatively, you can use a fresh apple or pear added before cooking if you want a smoother finish.

You can sprinkle nuts or seeds over just before serving. Serve with a little nut butter or almond milk and a bit of sweetener.

HolidayTraditional steel-cut oats

Serves 4

½ cup almond or soya milk

1 cup of distilled water

Pinch of fine salt

¼ teaspoon powdered cardamom

½ teaspoon powdered nutmeg

1 whole cinnamon sticks

½ cup traditional steel-cut oats

¼ cup nuts of your choosing, toasted and crushed

¼ cup cranberries, dried

¼ cup squash of your choice (I like pumpkin) cubed; or 1/4 cup of

Home-madepumpkin puree

Maple syrup

1 teaspoon pumpkin pie spice

Stir in the milk and water in your pot. Add the spices and seasoning. Stir in the cranberries. Finally add the pumpkin and the oats but do not stir these.

 Close your pot's lid.

If you are using an electronic cooker or an Instant Pot: Put it on the manual setting and choose a high pressure. Set the time for 3 minutes and allow the pressure to be naturally released.

If you have a manual cooker: Heat your stove plate to a medium-high heat and allow the pressure to build up until it is high. Then cook for 3 minutes. Let the pressure release naturally.

Take the lid off with care in case there is any steam left.

Stir well now. If you feel that it is too watery, put the lid on again and set aside for a few minutes.

Fish the cinnamon out. Dish up topped with extra pumpkin spice, maple syrup and the nuts.

Variation:
Use buckwheat groats in place the oats. Everything else is the same.

Steel-Cut, SavoryOatsin A Flash

Serves2

¼ cup scrubbed carrot, cubed

½ tablespoon of tamari

¼ cup onion or leek, chopped up nice and fine

¼ cup diced celery rib, sliced up nice and fine

1 garlic clove, skin removed and crushed

A pinch of pepper

¼ teaspoon paprika or chili powder

1¾ cups homemade veggie stock; or ¾ cuphome-made veggie stockand 1 cup almond or soya milk

½ cup sweet potato, cubed in bite-sized pieces

1 cup greens,cut up finely

½ cup traditional steel-cut oats

1 tablespoon miso

1 tablespoon nutritional yeast, as an additional extra

1 tablespoon parsley, flat-leafed or Italian, sliced up coarsely

2 teaspoons fresh lemon or lime juice

¼ cup scallions, sliced up nice and fine

If you are using an electronic cooker or an Instant Pot: Set it to "Sauté".

If you have a manual cooker: Heat your stove plate to a medium-high heat.

Put the celery, onion and carrot into your pot. Sauté for 3 minutes. Add in the garlic and the seasoning and fry for less than a minute.

Put in the liquid, the tamari and the potato. Mix in the oats and stir briefly.

Close your pot's lid.

If you are using an electronic cooker or an Instant Pot: Put it on the manual setting and choose

a high pressure. Set the time for 3 minutes and allow the pressure to be naturally released.

If you have a manual cooker: Heat your stove plate to a medium-high heat and allow the pressure to build up until it is high. Then cook for 3 minutes. Let the pressure release naturally.

Take the lid off with care in case there is any steam left.

Put in the yeast and the greens and stir quickly. Close the lid for a little bit so that the greens can wilt.

Add the lemon or lime juice and the miso just before serving. Serve using your scallions and parsley as a garnish. Eat immediately.

If you cook extra and are not planning to eat it all straight away, portion it before adding the miso. The miso must always be added just before the dish is served.

Chapter 2: Snacks

Bean Dip
Makes about 2½ cups

¾ cup homemade veggie stock

1 tablespoon coconut palm sugar; or a small date with the pit removed

1 cup raw cannellini beans, soak overnight in enough water to completely cover and then allow to drain for about half an hour before cooking

1 tablespoon miso

3 garlic cloves, skins removed and crushed

1 or 2 tablespoons of natural peanut butter

1 thumb-length piece of fresh ginger, peeled

1½ teaspoons of organic rice vinegar

About a tablespoon of fresh cilantro

1 scallion, sliced up nice and fine

Put the stock, 1 garlic clove, and beans into your cooker.

Close your pot's lid.

If you are using an electronic cooker or an Instant Pot: Put it on the manual setting and choose a high pressure. Set the time for 8 minutes and allow the pressure to be naturally released.

If you have a manual cooker: Heat your stove plate to a medium-high heat and allow the pressure to build up until it is high. Then cook for 8 minutes. Let the pressure release naturally.

Take the lid off with care in case there is any steam left.

Put the beans into a sieve or colander over a clean bowl so that the liquid drains off.

In your blender or food processor, blend together the garlic and ginger until fine. Add the beans with the peanut butter, the miso, vinegar and about 3 tablespoonsful of the liquid from cooking the beans. Blend until a chunky paste is formed. You can add more of the liquid from the beans if need be.

Add your sweetener, cilantro and the scallion and pulse shortly so it is just combined.

If need be, add more vinegar, sugar or miso.

This will last in the refrigerator for a total of 2-3 days. Alternatively, freeze on the day that you make it and keep for no longer than one month.

Wholesome Spread

Will make about 2 cups with a little bit extra

1 tablespoon sesame seeds

1 teaspoon cumin seeds, toasted and then ground up fine

4 to 5 medium scrubbed carrots, sliced into even pieces of about an inch

1 teaspoon fresh ginger, peeled and grated

2 tablespoons tahini

½ cup home-made veggie stockor distilled water

1 teaspoon dried ginger, finely ground

1 or 2 teaspoons of rice vinegar

Pepper

¼ to ½ teaspoon fine salt

If you are using an electronic cooker or an Instant Pot: Set it to "Sauté".

If you have a manual cooker: Heat your stove plate to a medium-high heat.

Take the lid off with care in case there is any steam left.

Put in the sesame seeds and allow them to fry for a bit until they can smell them cooking, stirring often. Put the fresh ginger in along with the cumin and stir to mix.

Put the stock in along with the carrots.

Close your pot's lid.

If you are using an electronic cooker or an Instant Pot: Put it on the manual setting and choose a high pressure. Set the time for 5 minutes and allow the pressure to be naturally released.

If you have a manual cooker: Heat your stove plate to a medium-high heat and allow the pressure to build up until it is high. Then cook for 5 minutes. Let the pressure release naturally.

Take the lid off with care in case there is any steam left.

Blend together the mixture, scraping down the sides of the blender from time to time. Add in any leftover ingredients and blend until it is completely smooth.

This is best served chilled so it should be refrigerated no less than an hour before it is ready to be served. It will last about 2-3 days in your refrigerator. It can be frozen for no longer than a month.

Eggplant Dip

Makes 1½ to 2 cups

3 tablespoons organic balsamic vinegar

2 pounds eggplant, skin removed and cubed

8 garlic cloves, skins removed and crushed

¼ cup tomatoes, sliced up nice and fine

2 tablespoons parsley, flat-leafed or Italian, sliced up coarsely

¼ cup homemade veggie stock

Fine salt and Pepper

2 tablespoons capers

1 teaspoon sugar; or 1 date pitted and soaked distilled water for at least an hour

2 tablespoons organically-sourced olive oil, as an optional extra

Toss together your eggplant and the vinegar. Set aside for a little while to allow it to infuse.

Put the eggplant mix, the stock and the garlic into your cooker.

Close your pot's lid.

If you are using an electronic cooker or an Instant Pot: Put it on the manual setting and choose a high pressure. Set the time for 2 minutes and allow the pressure to be naturally released.

If you have a manual cooker: Heat your stove plate to a medium-high heat and allow the pressure to build up until it is high. Then cook for 2 minutes. Let the pressure release naturally.

Take the lid off with care in case there is any steam left.

Move everything into a bowl. Put the leftover ingredients into the bowl and mix properly.

Set aside, covered, for a minimum of an hour.

You should get a distinct sweet and sour taste. If need be, you can add more seasonings, vinegar or sugar.

Baba Ganoush
Makes 2 cups

¼ cup homemade veggie stock

1½ to 2 pounds eggplant, skins removed and chopped into cubes

4 garlic cloves, skins removed and crushed

1 to 2 tablespoons of lemon or lime juice, to taste

2 tablespoons parsley, flat-leafed or Italian, sliced up coarsely

2 to 3 tablespoons tahini

Fine salt, as an optional extra

If you are using an electronic cooker or an Instant Pot: Set it to "Sauté".

If you have a manual cooker: Heat your stove plate to a medium-high heat.

Reserve one garlic clove and put the rest into your pot along with a tablespoon of stock. Fry a little while.

Pour in the remaining stock and the eggplants.

Close your pot's lid.

If you are using an electronic cooker or an Instant Pot: Put it on the manual setting and choose a high pressure. Set the time for 2 minutes and allow the pressure to be naturally released.

If you have a manual cooker: Heat your stove plate to a medium-high heat and allow the pressure to build up until it is high. Then cook for 2 minutes. Let the pressure release naturally.

Take the lid off with care in case there is any steam left.

Make sure your eggplant is completely cooked. If not, put under pressure again for a minute to finish the cooking.

Blend or process the eggplant along with the remaining garlic, the lemon or lime juice, the parsley and the tahini until it is just slightly chunky.

If you are choosing to use salt, do so now.

You can either serve straight away or chill before serving. It can be stored for about 3-4 days in your refrigerator. It will last in the freezer for about a month if frozen on the day it was made.

Bean Dip with Some Kick

½ cup red or yellow bell pepper, sliced up nice and fine

1 cup raw white beans that have been soaked in enough water to cover them overnight and then drained at least half an hour before you start to cook (retain the liquid)

¾ cup homemade veggie stock

1¾ teaspoons thyme, it is best to use dried

½ teaspoon sage, it is best to use dried

1 tablespoon of lemon or lime juice

½ teaspoon fine salt

1 tablespoon organically-sourced olive oil, optional

Parsley, fresh flat-leafed or Italian, sliced up coarsely, for garnish

½ teaspoon pepper if you want to add it

Mix together your sage, half the thyme, stock, beans and bell pepper in your pot.

Close your pot's lid.

If you are using an electronic cooker or an Instant Pot: Put it on the manual setting and choose a high pressure. Set the time for 8 minutes and allow the pressure to be naturally released.

If you have a manual cooker: Heat your stove plate to a medium-high heat and allow the pressure to build up until it is high. Then cook for 8 minutes. Let the pressure release naturally.

Take the lid off with care in case there is any steam left.

Reserve the parsley. Allow the beans to cool a little before processing them along with the remaining ingredients until they form a smooth paste. (Add some of the reserved water from the beans if it is too thick.)

Apple Chutney
Makes 1 pint

2 cups of onions,chopped up nice and fine

3 cups of tart apples (or a mixture of equal parts pears and apples)

1 Jalapeño, chopped up nice and fine (if you like it fiery, leave in the seeds, otherwise remove the seeds before chopping)

¾ to 1 cup organic apple cider vinegar

1 cup of currants or raisins

½ cup sugar, brown has a nicer taste here

1 tablespoon of mustard seeds

1 or 2 teaspoons ginger, peeled and freshly grated

½ or 1 teaspoon fine salt

Mix together each of the ingredients, reserving only the salt. Stir them together in.

Close your pot's lid.

If you are using an electronic cooker or an Instant Pot: Put it on the manual setting and choose a high pressure. Set the time for 5 minutes and allow the pressure to be naturally released.

If you have a manual cooker: Heat your stove plate to a medium-high heat and allow the pressure to build up until it is high. Then cook for 5 minutes. Let the pressure release naturally.

Take the lid off with care in case there is any steam left.

Add the salt when done and then can as you normally would.

Biryani
Serves 2

½ cup scrubbed carrot, chopped up nice and fine

½ cup green beans, chopped up nice and fine

½ cup sweet potato, chopped up nice and fine

½ cup cauliflower, chopped up nice and fine

1 tablespoon lime or lemon or lime juice

1½ garlic cloves, skins removed and crushed

½ small jalapeño, chopped up nice and fine (deseed to reduce some of the fiery taste)

½ teaspoon ginger, peeled and freshly grated

1 cupand a separate⅓ cup homemade veggie stock

½ tablespoon oil as an optional extra

¾ cup onion, chopped up nice and fine

¼ cup chopped tomatoes

½ teaspoon cumin seeds

¾ teaspoons garam masala: if possible, go to your local spice shop and get it made up freshly

½ teaspoon turmeric powder

½ cup raw brown basmati rice: soak it for at least an hour in enough water to cover it and then drain well before cooking

1 small bay leaf

1 tablespoon fresh cilantro, chopped up nice and fine

Fine salt

Mix the vegetables together in one dish.

In a separate bowl, mix the garlic, jalapenos, ginger and the lemon or lime juice.

Mix into the veggies, ensuring that they are completely coated. Set aside for about 15-20 minutes.

Put this mixture into your pot along with the ⅓cup of stock.

Close your pot's lid.

If you are using an electronic cooker or an Instant Pot: Put it on the manual setting and choose a high pressure. Set the time for 2 minutes and allow the pressure to be naturally released.

If you have a manual cooker: Heat your stove plate to a medium-high heat and allow the pressure to build up until it is high. Then cook for 2 minutes. Let the pressure release naturally.

Take the lid off with care in case there is any steam left.

Take it out of your pot and put it on one side.

If you are using an electronic cooker or an Instant Pot: Set it to "Sauté".

If you have a manual cooker: Heat your stove plate to a medium-high heat.

If you are using the oil, now is the time to add it. Fry your onion quickly until it has started to soften up.

Add the remaining herbs and spices, the reserved stock, the tomatoes and the rice.

Close your pot's lid.

If you are using an electronic cooker or an Instant Pot: Put it on the manual setting and choose a high pressure. Set the time for 15 minutes and allow the pressure to be naturally released.

If you have a manual cooker: Heat your stove plate to a medium-high heat and allow the pressure to build up until it is high. Then cook for 15 minutes. Let the pressure release naturally.

Take the lid off with care in case there is any steam left.

Stir in the vegetables along with any of their juices.

Close the lid and allow the veggies to warm through in the pot's residual heat for a few minutes.

Take out the bay leaf, and garnish with extra cilantro.

Polenta with Herbs

Serves 2

1 tablespoon organically-sourced olive oil as an optional extra

¼ cup onion, chopped up nice and fine

1 teaspoon garlic cloves, skins removed and crushed

2 cups home-made veggie stockor distilled water

½ teaspoon fine salt

1 small bay leaf

1 teaspoon fresh oregano, chopped up nice and fine

½ teaspoon fresh rosemary, chopped up nice and fine

1½ tablespoons fresh basil, chopped up nice and fine

1 tablespoons parsley, flat-leafed or Italian, sliced up coarsely

½ cup coarse polenta

If you are using an electronic cooker or an Instant Pot: Set it to "Sauté".

If you have a manual cooker: Heat your stove plate to a medium-high heat.

If you are using the oil, now is the time to add it. Put the onion into your pot and fry while stirring continuously for around a minute. Add the garlic and fry it for just under a minute.

Put the water, bay lead, rosemary, oregano and salt into your pot. Reserve half of the parsley and basil and pit the rest into the pot. Stir so that everything becomes incorporated.

Distribute the polenta evenly throughout the pot but do not stir it.

Close your pot's lid.

If you are using an electronic cooker or an Instant Pot: Put it on the manual setting and choose a high pressure. Set the time for 5 minutes and allow the pressure to be naturally released.

If you have a manual cooker: Heat your stove plate to a medium-high heat and allow the pressure to build up until it is high. Then cook for 5 minutes. Let the pressure release naturally.

Take the lid off with care in case there is any steam left.

Find what's left of the bay leaf and put it in the bin. Whisk up the polenta mixture until it is free of lumps. If the mixture is too watery, leave the lid on for a bit.

You can serve as a side dish or snack. Alternatively, you can let it cool down and then grill or fry it till it crisps up.

Sorghumfor Energy

Serves 2

1/2 cup onion, chopped up nice and fine

1/2 cup sorghum

1/4 cup apricots, dried and chopped up nice and fine

1 1/4 cups of distilled water or home-made veggie broth

½ teaspoon fine salt, as an optional extra

1/4 cup lightly toasted almonds, cut into wafer-thin slivers

¼ cup orange, lemon or lime juice

1 tablespoon mint, fresh and coarsely chopped to use as a garnish

If you are using an electronic cooker or an Instant Pot: Set it to "Sauté".

If you have a manual cooker: Heat your stove plate to a medium-high heat.

Put in the onion and fry it up for a little. Mix in the sorghum grains and cook for about 10-15 seconds. Stir half of the apricots in along with the distilled water. If you want to use salt, now is the time.

Close your pot's lid.

If you are using an electronic cooker or an Instant Pot: Put it on the manual setting and choose a high pressure. Set the time for 35 minutes and allow the pressure to be naturally released.

If you have a manual cooker: Heat your stove plate to a medium-high heat and allow the pressure to build up until it is high. Then cook for 35 minutes. Let the pressure release naturally.

Take the lid off with care in case there is any steam left.

Take the sorghum out of your pot and into a big bowl. Put in the rest of the apricots along with the nuts. Then stir the juice throughout the mixture.

You can serve as is garnished with the mint or let it cool a little first.

Risotto Without the Rice

Serves 2

1 onion,chopped up nice and fine

½ tablespoon organically-sourced olive oil

1 clove garlic, skin removed and crushed

1 bay leaf

¾ cups buckwheat groats (You might also know them by the name of Kasha)

1 cup mushrooms, sliced up nice and fine

2 cups home-made veggie or mushroom stock

1 tablespoon ground dried porcini or shiitake mushrooms (they have an intense flavor so a little goes a long way)

1½ tablespoons parsley, flat-leafed or Italian, sliced up coarsely

Fine salt

1 teaspoon balsamic vinegar

If you are using an electronic cooker or an Instant Pot: Set it to "Sauté".

If you have a manual cooker: Heat your stove plate to a medium-high heat.

Put the oil in the pot and follow up with the onion. Let the onion fry for a bit until it becomes transparent.

Add in the garlic, followed by the buckwheat.

Stir well so that everything is coated in oil.

Put the bay leaf in and follow with both lots of mushrooms.

Cook for about two or three minutes before adding in the stock.

Close your pot's lid.

If you are using an electronic cooker or an Instant Pot: Put it on the manual setting and choose a high pressure. Set the time for 3 minutes and allow the pressure to be naturally released.

If you have a manual cooker: Heat your stove plate to a medium-high heat and allow the pressure to build up until it is high. Then cook for 3 minutes. Let the pressure release naturally.

Take the lid off with care in case there is any steam left.

Put the vinegar in your pot and mix it all up properly. If you feel that the mixture is too thick, add a bit more stock.

If you feel that the mixture is not thick enough, sauté it for a few minutes.

Take out the bay leaf. Put the parsley in and check to see if any more seasoning should be added.

Chapter 3: Lunch

Curried Burgers

Makes 4 burgers

2 tablespoons brown rice

¼ cup black rice

1 cup of distilled water or homemade veggie stock

2 garlic cloves, skins removed and crushed

½ cup raw kidney beans, soak them overnight and drain about a half an hour before you want to cook them

½ tablespoon and an extra 1 teaspoon mild curry powder

Vegan cooking spray, as an optional extra

½ cup of distilled water

2 tablespoons scallions, sliced well

½ tablespoon of lemon or lime juice

¼ cup tomato, cut up into small cubes

¼ cup hemp seeds

½ teaspoon fine salt

½ tablespoon black mustard seeds

½ cup kale leaves, pack them tightly

Mix together both lots of rice with the water/ stock in your pot.

Close your pot's lid.

If you are using an electronic cooker or an Instant Pot: Put it on the manual setting and choose a high pressure. Set the time for 200 minutes and allow the pressure to be naturally released.

If you have a manual cooker: Heat your stove plate to a medium-high heat and allow the pressure to build up until it is high. Then cook for 20 minutes. Let the pressure release naturally.

Take the lid off with care in case there is any steam left.

Remove your cooked rice and put it out of the way.

Mix together the beans, the ½ tablespoon of curry powder, a half cup of distilled water and half of the garlic in your pot.

Close your pot's lid.

If you are using an electronic cooker or an Instant Pot: Put it on the manual setting and choose a high pressure. Set the time for 7 minutes and allow the pressure to be naturally released.

If you have a manual cooker: Heat your stove plate to a medium-high heat and allow the pressure to build up until it is high. Then cook for 7 minutes. Let the pressure release naturally.

Put the beans into another bowl.

Set your oven's temperature at 375°F. Line a large baking tray with baking paper.

Mix half of the rice with half of the beans. To this add the leftover garlic along with the scallions, the tomato, the hemp seeds, the lemon or lime juice, and the kale.

Process until blended but still a little crunchy.

Mix in the remaining ingredients with a spoon and set aside a little while.

Wet your hands with cold water and divide the mixture into 4 evenly sized portions. Make patties out of them.

Lay out on the baking tray and cook for around 10-15 minutes on each side.

Potato Burgers

Makes 4 burgers

1 teaspoon of ginger, freshly peeled and then ground

½ cup onion, chopped up nice and fine

½ cup fresh, strongly flavored mushrooms, like shiitake, cleaned and destemmed

½ cup red lentils, thoroughly rinsed and cleaned

1 sweet potato, scrubbed, peeled and cubed

2 tablespoonsof hemp seeds

1¼ cups homemade veggie stock

Vegan cooking spray as an optional extra

½ tablespoon medium to hot curry powder

2 tablespoons parsley, flat-leafed or Italian, sliced up coarsely

1 tablespoon brown rice flour, if the mixture is too sloppy

½ cup quick cooking oats

2 tablespoons cilantro, sliced up nice and fine

If you are using an electronic cooker or an Instant Pot: Set it to "Sauté".

If you have a manual cooker: Heat your stove plate to a medium-high heat.

Place the mushrooms, ginger and onion in and allow them to cook for a minute or so. Add in the stock, along with your lentils and the sweet potato.

Close your pot's lid.

If you are using an electronic cooker or an Instant Pot: Put it on the manual setting and choose a high pressure. Set the time for 6 minutes and allow the pressure to be naturally released.

If you have a manual cooker: Heat your stove plate to a medium-high heat and allow the pressure to build up until it is high. Then cook for 6 minutes. Let the pressure release naturally.

Take the lid off with care in case there is any steam left.

Set it all aside until it cools down.

Set your oven temperature to 375°F. Take a large oven dish and line it using baking paper.

Mash the lentils and mix the hemp into the mash. Add the parsley, curry powder and cilantro. Mix in the oats.

You should be left with a paste that is rather thick and that can be shaped. If it is too sloppy, you can add some of the flour.

Wet your hands with cool water and divide the mixture into four equal portions. Shape them into patties.

Arrange your patties onto the prepared oven dish and set in the oven for ten minutes per side.

These burgers freeze well.

Arroz non Pollo

Serves 2

1¼ cups homemade veggie stock

1½ garlic cloves, skins removed and crushed cloves, skins removed and crushed

½ cup sliced cremini or shiitake mushrooms

Pinch of cayenne

½ bunch cilantro

¼ cup frozen peas

½ cup scrubbed carrot, cut into julienne strips

½ teaspoon turmeric or a pinch of saffron

¼ cup diced red bell pepper

Pinch of crushed red pepper flakes

1 cup brown rice

¼ cup pinto beans, soaked and drained

Fine salt and Pepper

¼ cup corn kernels, if using frozen, thaw first

Put the cilantroin a blender and whizz until smooth.

If you are using an electronic cooker or an Instant Pot: Set it to "Sauté".

If you have a manual cooker: Heat your stove plate to a medium-high heat.

Add the mushrooms and fry up until they begin to soften. Add the scrubbed carrot, garlic cloves, skins removed and crushed, turmeric, cayenneand red pepper, stir well, and cook for 1 more minute.

Add the blended cilantro, brownrice, and drained beans. Stir.

Close your pot's lid.

If you are using an electronic cooker or an Instant Pot: Put it on the manual setting and choose a high pressure. Set the time for 20 minutes and allow the pressure to be naturally released.

If you have a manual cooker: Heat your stove plate to a medium-high heat and allow the pressure to build up until it is high. Then cook for 20 minutes. Let the pressure release naturally.

Add the bell pepper, peas, and corn. Shut the lid of your pot again and leave off the heat for a few minutes.

Add fine salt and pepper if you prefer. Transfer to a platter and serve.

Chapter 4: Dinner

Curried Vegetables

Serves 2

1 cup onion, chopped up nice and fine

½ cup chopped frozen cooked eggplant, thawed

1 teaspoon curry powder

1½ garlic cloves, skins removed and crushed

1 teaspoon ground toasted cumin

½ teaspoon ground cinnamon

½ cup homemade veggie stock

1 cup cooked white or other beans

1½tablespoons fresh orange juice

1½ tablespoons tomato paste

1 cup chopped greens, such as turnip, mustard, or kale

½ cup tomatoes, chopped up nice and fine

1 large date, sliced

1 tablespoon chopped fresh cilantro or parsley, flat-leafed or Italian, sliced up coarsely, optional

If you are using an electronic cooker or an Instant Pot: Set it to "Sauté".

If you have a manual cooker: Heat your stove plate to a medium-high heat.

Add the onion and dry sauté for 3 minutes. Add the garlic cloves, curry powder, cumin, and cinnamon and cook for 2 minutes longer, adding some of the stock, a tablespoon at a time, if anything starts to stick.

Add the stock, beans, eggplant, tomatoes, and date.

If you are using an electronic cooker or an Instant Pot: Put it on the manual setting and choose a high pressure. Set the time for 2 minutes and release the pressure quickly.

If you have a manual cooker: Heat your stove plate to a medium-high heat and allow the pressure to build up until it is high. Then cook for 2 minutes. And allow the pressure to be quickly released

Take the lid off with care in case there is any steam left.

Add in your greens and your tomato paste. Do not stir.

Close your pot's lid.

If you are using an electronic cooker or an Instant Pot: Put it on the manual setting and choose a high pressure. Set the time for 1 minute and release the pressure quickly.

If you have a manual cooker: Heat your stove plate to a medium-high heat and allow the pressure to build up until it is high. Then cook for 1 minute. And allow the pressure to be quickly released

Take the lid off with care in case there is any steam left.

Stir contents and add the orange juice. Transfer to a bowl. Serve garnished with cilantro or parsley, flat-leafed or Italian, sliced up coarsely, if available.

Bean and Potato Mash Up

Serves 2

½ cup onion,chopped up nice and fine

½ tablespoon oil, optional

1 clovegarlic, skins removed and crushed

1 teaspoonchili powder as hot as you like it

1 cup sweet potatoes, peeled and cubed

⅓ cup homemade veggie stock

¼ cup scallions, chopped

½ cup black beans, pre-cooked

¼ teaspoon fine salt

Chopped cilantro, to serve as garnish

Splash of any hot sauce, as an optional extra

If you are using an electronic cooker or an Instant Pot: Set it to "Sauté".

If you have a manual cooker: Heat your stove plate to a medium-high heat.

If you are using the oil, now would be the time to add it.

Put in your onion and let it cook for 2 to 3 minutes. Add the garlic cloves, skins removed and crushed and stir. Put in the potatoes and the chili seasoning. Make sure that the potatoes get a good coating of the seasoning.

Add the stockand stir.

Close your pot's lid.

If you are using an electronic cooker or an Instant Pot: Put it on the manual setting and choose

a high pressure. Set the time for 3 minutes and allow the pressure to be naturally released.

If you have a manual cooker: Heat your stove plate to a medium-high heat and allow the pressure to build up until it is high. Then cook for 3 minutes. Let the pressure release naturally.

Take the lid off with care in case there is any steam left.

Put in the scallions along with the black beans and add more salt if you want to.

Close up the lid and let the beans warm through in the residual heat from the cooker.

Add hot sauce, if desired. Taste and add more fine salt, if you like. Serve with the cilantro over it.

Tofu and Squash Casserole

Serves 2

½ cup onion chopped up nice and fine

1 tablespoon Cajun seasoning blend

1 tablespoon tamari or Bragg liquid aminos

½ pound extra firm vacuum packed tofu, drained and cubed

¼ cup diced celery rib, sliced up nice and fine

½ tablespoon red wine vinegar

¼ cup diced bell pepper

½ small jalapeño

¼ cup homemade veggie stock

½ tablespoon minced garlic cloves, skins removed and crushed

½ cup diced eggplant

½ cup sliced okra

Chopped fresh flat-leaf parsley, flat-leafed or Italian, sliced up coarsely, for garnish

½ cup diced summer squash, any color

Place the tofu into a clean dish that has a lid. Sprinkle the spices over it.

Drizzle on 1 tablespoon of the tamari and the vinegar. Stir so that all of the tofu is coveredwith seasoning. Set to one side and cover the mix. Leave for at least an hour.

If you are using an electronic cooker or an Instant Pot: Set it to "Sauté".

If you have a manual cooker: Heat your stove plate to a medium-high heat.

Add the finely chopped onion and celery rib, sliced up nice and fine, and dry sauté for 2 minutes. Add the bell pepper, jalapenos, if using, and garlic cloves, and sauté 1 minute longer. Add the tofu and stir.

Add the eggplant, okraand summer squash; do not stir.

Add the stock to the pot.

Close your pot's lid.

If you are using an electronic cooker or an Instant Pot: Put it on the manual setting and choose a high pressure. Set the time for 3 minutes and release the pressure quickly.

If you have a manual cooker: Heat your stove plate to a medium-high heat and allow the pressure to build up until it is high. Then cook for 3 minutes. And allow the pressure to be quickly released

Take the lid off with care in case there is any steam left.

Transfer to a bowl or platter. Drizzle with the remaining 1 tablespoon tamari and garnishwith parsley.

Collard Rollswith Mushrooms and Oats

Serves 2

½ cup mushrooms, sliced up fine

¼ cup leek, sliced up fine

1½ garlic cloves, skins removed and crushed

½ cup oat groats:let them soak overnight and then drain them well

½ cup of distilled water

1 teaspoon of Italian seasoning

1 cup homemade veggie stock

4 ounces can tomato sauce

If you are using an electronic cooker or an Instant Pot: Set it to "Sauté".

If you have a manual cooker: Heat your stove plate to a medium-high heat.

Add the collard stems, mushrooms, and leek and dry sauté for 3 minutes. Put the seasoning and garlic in and fry for no longer than a minute.

Add the drained oat groats and stock.

Close your pot's lid.

If you are using an electronic cooker or an Instant Pot: Put it on the manual setting and choose a high pressure. Set the time for 20 minutes and allow the pressure to be naturally released.

If you have a manual cooker: Heat your stove plate to a medium-high heat and allow the pressure to build up until it is high. Then cook for 20 minutes. Let the pressure release naturally.

Take the lid off with care in case there is any steam left.

Transfer everything into a relatively big bowl.

Let the filling sit until it's cool enough to handle.

Wash the pressure cooker. Add 1 cup of distilled water and a trivet or rack to elevate the dish abovethe water.

When you are able to handle the filling, lay out a collard leaf and add about ½ cupfilling. Roll the sides in and roll up like a spring roll.

Put the completed roll into a liddeddish that fits inside the pressure cooker.

Fill all the leaves.

Combine the tomato sauce and ½ cup of distilled water. Pour over the collard rolls. Cover the dish with its lid before putting into your pot.

Close your pot's lid.

If you are using an electronic cooker or an Instant Pot: Put it on the manual setting and choose a high pressure. Set the time for 3 minutes and allow the pressure to be naturally released.

If you have a manual cooker: Heat your stove plate to a medium-high heat and allow the pressure to build up until it is high. Then cook for 3 minutes. Let the pressure release naturally.

Take the lid off with care in case there is any steam left.

Veggie Chili
Serves 2

2 garlic cloves, skins removed and crushed cloves

½ cup diced cremini mushrooms

1 cup onion, sliced up nice and fine

½ cup diced scrubbed carrot

½ small jalapeño, seeded (or not, if you prefermore heat) and sliced up nice and finely

½ tablespoon paprika or mild chili powder

¾ cup brown, green, black, or French green lentils, thoroughly rinsed

½ teaspoon chili powder

¼ cup split red lentils, thoroughly rinsed

1 cup homemade veggie stock

7.5 ounces diced tomatoes

¾ cups winter squash, diced

Hot sauce, as required

1 tablespoon tomato paste

Fine salt and Pepper if you want to add it

If you are using an electronic cooker or an Instant Pot: Set it to "Sauté".

If you have a manual cooker: Heat your stove plate to a medium-high heat.

Add the onion, mushrooms, and scrubbed carrot and dry sauté for2 minutes.

Add the garlic, jalapenos, paprika, and chili powder and cook 1 minute longer.

Add both kinds oflentils, thewinter squash, and stock. Stir once.

Close your pot's lid.

If you are using an electronic cooker or an Instant Pot: Put it on the manual setting and choose a high pressure. Set the time for 6 minutes and allow the pressure to be naturally released.

If you have a manual cooker: Heat your stove plate to a medium-high heat and allow the pressure to build up until it is high. Then cook for 6 minutes. Let the pressure release naturally.

Take the lid off with care in case there is any steam left.

Add the tomatoes along with the tomato paste. Stir.

Shut the lid and set aside for a few minutes.

Season if you like.

Tofu a la Mediterranean
Serves 2

½ tablespoon organically-sourced olive oil, optional

½ cup mild onion, chopped up nice and fine

½ teaspoon rosemary, fresh and sliced up nice and fine

1½ garlic cloves, skins removed and crushed

1 mild bell pepper, julienned

1 bay leaf

½ pound tofu, cubed

¼ cup homemade veggie stock

1 tablespoon red wine vinegar

5 Kalamata olives, chopped up finely

½ tablespoon tomato paste

Fine salt and Pepper

1 tablespoon parsley, sliced upcoarsely, or basil

If you are using an electronic cooker or an Instant Pot: Set it to "Sauté".

If you have a manual cooker: Heat your stove plate to a medium-high heat.

Addthe olive oil, if using. Add in the onion andpeppers and cook for 3 minutes.

Add the garlic, rosemary, and bay leaves and cook another 30 seconds.

Add the vinegar and tofu and stir. Add the stock and stir again. Drop the tomato paste into the pot but don't stir it in.

Close your pot's lid.

If you are using an electronic cooker or an Instant Pot: Put it on the manual setting and choose

a high pressure. Set the time for 3 minutes and allow the pressure to be naturally released.

If you have a manual cooker: Heat your stove plate to a medium-high heat and allow the pressure to build up until it is high. Then cook for 3 minutes. Let the pressure release naturally.

Take the lid off with care in case there is any steam left.

Stir in the olives and chopped herbs. Close your lid and let the mixture cook in the residual heat for about 5 minutes or so.

Remove your bay leaves. Season and serve.

Chapter 5: Side Dishes

New-Style Brussel Sprouts

Serves 2

1 teaspoon of lemon or lime juice

½ medium unpeeled apple, cut into bite-sized pieces

1 teaspoon canola or pure sesame oil, optional

1½ cups Brussels sprouts, cut in half or quarters

¼ cup sliced up nice and fine leek

½ teaspoon thyme, it is best to use dried

¼ cup home-made veggie stockor distilled water

1 teaspoon balsamic vinegar

½ tablespoon tamari or Bragg Liquid Aminos

Parsley, flat-leafed or Italian, sliced up coarsely

Pepper if you want to add it

Toss the apple with the lemon or lime juice in a small bowl and set aside.

If you are using an electronic cooker or an Instant Pot: Set it to "Sauté".

If you have a manual cooker: Heat your stove plate to a medium-high heat.

If you are using the oil, now is the time to add it.

Sauté the leek for 1 minute, so that it begins to get softer.

Add the apple, Brussels sprouts, and thyme. Stir. Add the tamari and stock. Stir.

Close your pot's lid.

If you are using an electronic cooker or an Instant Pot: Put it on the manual setting and choose a low pressure. Set the time for 3 minutes and release the pressure quickly.

If you have a manual cooker: Heat your stove plate to a medium-high heat and allow the pressure to build up until it is low. Then cook for 3 minutes. And allow the pressure to be quickly released

Take the lid off with care in case there is any steam left.

Stir in the balsamic vinegar and pepper. Transfer the vegetables to a bowl orplatter.

Parsnipsto Die For

Serves 2

¾ pound parsnips, cubed

¼ cup homemade veggie stock

1½ tablespoons balsamic vinegar

1 tablespoon maple syrup

Fine salt and Pepper

Combine the parsnips, vinegar and stock, in your pot.

Close your pot's lid.

If you are using an electronic cooker or an Instant Pot: Put it on the manual setting and choose a high pressure. Set the time for 3 minutes and release the pressure quickly.

If you have a manual cooker: Heat your stove plate to a medium-high heat and allow the pressure to build up until it is high. Then cook for 3 minutes. And allow the pressure to be quickly released

Take the lid off with care in case there is any steam left.

Check to see that the parsnips are fully tender. If not and they need more liquid,add afew more tablespoons of stock or distilled water.

Close your pot's lid.

If you are using an electronic cooker or an Instant Pot: Put it on the manual setting and choose a high pressure. Set the time for 1 minute and release the pressure quickly.

If you have a manual cooker: Heat your stove plate to a medium-high heat and allow the pressure to build up until it is high. Then cook for 1 minute. And allow the pressure to be quickly released

Stir in the maple syrup and season to taste with fine salt and pepper.

Broccoli Mushroom Mix

Serves 2

1½ garlic cloves, skins removed and crushed cloves, skins removed and crushed

¼ cup diced chopped up nice and fine

½ teaspoon minced fresh ginger

½ pound broccoli

4 ounces cremini or oyster mushrooms, sliced

1 tablespoon tamari

1 tablespoon homemade veggie stock

1 tablespoon toasted sesame seeds, to use as a decoration

If you are using an electronic cooker or an Instant Pot: Set it to "Sauté".

If you have a manual cooker: Heat your stove plate to a medium-high heat.

Add the onion and garlic, along with the ginger and let it fry for no more than a minute.

Add the mushrooms, broccoli, stock, and tamari.

Close your pot's lid.

If you are using an electronic cooker or an Instant Pot: Put it on the manual setting and choose a low pressure. Set the time for 1 minute and release the pressure quickly.

If you have a manual cooker: Heat your stove plate to a medium-high heat and allow the pressure to build up until it is low. Then cook for 1 minute. And allow the pressure to be quickly released

Take the lid off with care in case there is any steam left.

Chapter 6: Sauces and Soups

A lot of the recipes in this chapter are double up recipes. Freeze the rest for another meal.

Rich Veggie Stock
Makes 2 quarts

2 red onions, chopped up nice and fine

1 tablespoon oil, optional

3 garlic cloves, skins removed and crushed, smashed

½ cup shiitake mushroom stems, or 4 whole dried shiitake mushrooms

2 scrubbed carrots, scrubbed well and coarsely chopped

6 ounces cremini or shiitake mushrooms, sliced

8 cups of distilled water

2 celery rib, sliced up nice and fine stalks with leaves, chopped

1 sprig rosemary

2 bay leaves

½ teaspoon fine salt

3 sprigs thyme

¼ teaspoon whole black peppercorns

If you are using an electronic cooker or an Instant Pot: Set it to "Sauté".

If you have a manual cooker: Heat your stove plate to a medium-high heat.

Add the oil, if using. Put the onion in and cook for 4 minutes.

Add the garlic and cook until the onion begins to get caramelized. Add all the remaining ingredients except the fine salt.

Close your pot's lid.

If you are using an electronic cooker or an Instant Pot: Put it on the manual setting and choose a high pressure. Set the time for 10 minutes and allow the pressure to be naturally released.

If you have a manual cooker: Heat your stove plate to a medium-high heat and allow the pressure to build up until it is high. Then cook for 10 minutes. Let the pressure release naturally.

Take the lid off with care in case there is any steam left.

Strain the stock by pouring through a strainer and pressing on the solids with aspoon toextract all the liquid and flavor.

 Add the fine salt to the stock.

Mushroom Stock

Makes 6 cups

6 ounces cremini mushrooms, diced

2 cups onion or leeks, sliced up nice and fine

8 to 12 dried shiitake mushrooms, plus any additional fresh mushroom stems

8 cups of distilled water

½ ounce dried wild mushroom mix

2 tablespoons porcini powder

1 teaspoon fresh thyme, optional

1 teaspoon black peppercorns

2 bay leaves

If you are using an electronic cooker or an Instant Pot: Set it to "Sauté".

If you have a manual cooker: Heat your stove plate to a medium-high heat.

Add the chopped up nice and fine and fresh mushrooms. Fry until the mushrooms have started to soften up.

Add the remainingingredients.

Close your pot.

If you are using an electronic cooker or an Instant Pot: Put it on the manual setting and choose a high pressure. Set the time for 5 minutes and allow the pressure to be naturally released.

If you have a manual cooker: Heat your stove plate to a medium-high heat and allow the pressure to build up until it is high. Then cook for 5 minutes. Let the pressure release naturally.

Take the lid off with care in case there is any steam left.

Carefully strain the stock and extract as much liquid and flavor as possible.

Note: You can buy porcini or shiitake mushroom powder or make yourown bygrinding dried mushrooms in a spice grinder until smooth.

Onion Soup
Makes 7 cups

1 onion, slicedup nice and fine

Vegan cooking spray/ 1 teaspoon oil

1 leek, cleaned well and sliced

1 sprig fresh sage or 1 teaspoon dried sage

2 tablespoons garlic cloves, skins removed and

3 sprigs parsley, flat-leafed or Italian, sliced up coarsely

2 teaspoons black peppercorns

Fine salt and powdered black pepper

1 sprig fresh thyme

If you are using an electronic cooker or an Instant Pot: Set it to "Sauté".

If you have a manual cooker: Heat your stove plate to a medium-high heat.

Spray with cooking spray or add the oil. Add onion, the leek, and garlic and fry a bit until soft. Add 8 cups of distilled water, the herbs, and the peppercorns.

Close the lid of your pot.

If you are using an electronic cooker or an Instant Pot: Put it on the manual setting and choose a high pressure. Set the time for 5 minutes and allow the pressure to be naturally released.

If you have a manual cooker: Heat your stove plate to a medium-high heat and allow the pressure to build up until it is high. Then cook for 5 minutes. Let the pressure release naturally.

Take the lid off with care in case there is any steam left.

Strain the solids out of the soup or blend until smooth for a heartier meal.

Season as you want to.

Tomato Soup with Heart
Serves 6 to 8

2 cups onion, chopped up nice and fine

1 tablespoon organically-sourced olive oil, optional

2 to 3 tablespoons garlic cloves, skins removed and crushed

2 tablespoons Italian seasoning

2 bay leaves

1½ cups dried white beans, soaked and drained

3 cups homemade veggie stock

¼ cup sliced up nice and fine sun-dried tomatoes

1½ cups tomatoes, sliced up nice and fine

½ medium green cabbage, cut into 1- to 2-inch pieces

Fine salt to taste or a splash of vinegar, optional

Chopped fresh basil leaves, if available

If you are using an electronic cooker or an Instant Pot: Set it to "Sauté".

If you have a manual cooker: Heat your stove plate to a medium-high heat.

Addthe oil, if using.

Add the onionand cook gently until it begins to soften. Add half the garlic, the bay leaves, andItalian seasoning and sauté 1 minute longer.

(Ifusing an electric cooker, turn off sauté now.)

Add the beans, sun-dried tomatoesand stock.

Close the lid of your pot.

If you are using an electronic cooker or an Instant Pot: Put it on the manual setting and choose a high pressure. Set the time for 10 minutes and allow the pressure to be naturally released.

If you have a manual cooker: Heat your stove plate to a medium-high heat and allow the pressure to build up until it is high. Then cook for 10 minutes. Let the pressure release naturally.

Take the lid off with care in case there is any steam left.

Add the cabbage, tomatoes, and remaining garlic.

Close the lid of your pot.

If you are using an electronic cooker or an Instant Pot: Put it on the manual setting and choose a high pressure. Set the time for 5 minutes and allow the pressure to be naturally released.

If you have a manual cooker: Heat your stove plate to a medium-high heat and allow the pressure to build up until it is high. Then cook for 5 minutes. Let the pressure release naturally.

Take the lid off with care in case there is any steam left.

Remove and discard the bay leaves with tongs.

Add the fine salt or vinegar to thesoup, if youlike, and garnish each bowl with a few chopped basilleaves.

Gourmet Cabbage Soup

Serves 4

1 cup finely diced onion

2 teaspoons canola oil, optional

1 jalapeño, either dried and left whole, or freshand minced, as an optional extra

1 garlic clove, skin removed and crushed

1 lemongrass stalk, hard outer leaves discarded, stalk trimmed, cut into 2-inchpieces, and bruised with the back ofa knife

2 thin slices fresh ginger, about the size of a quarter, plus more for grating

1 medium Yukon Gold or other potato, sliced up

Grated zest and juice of either a lemon or a lime

½ medium to large cabbage, thinly sliced

4 cups homemade veggie broth

Fresh chopped cilantro, for garnish

½ cup coconut milk, coconut distilled water, or coconut beverage, or a few dropscoconut extract mixed with distilled water or stock

Fine salt and Pepper if you want to add it

If you are using an electronic cooker or an Instant Pot: Set it to "Sauté".

If you have a manual cooker: Heat your stove plate to a medium-high heat.

Add the oil, if using. Add the onion and cook for 1 to 2 minutes, until no longer raw.

Add thejalapenos, if using, the lemongrass, garlic, and ginger, and cook another minute or two, until the onion is just beginning to soften.

Add the sliced cabbage and potato, along with the stock and coconut milk.

Close the lid of your pot.

If you are using an electronic cooker or an Instant Pot: Put it on the manual setting and choose a high pressure. Set the time for 4 minutes and allow the pressure to be naturally released.

If you have a manual cooker: Heat your stove plate to a medium-high heat and allow the pressure to build up until it is high. Then cook for 4 minutes. Let the pressure release naturally.

Take the lid off with care in case there is any steam left.

Using tongs, remove and discard the dried jalapenos, if using, along with the gingerandlemongrass pieces.

Add lime zest and juice to taste and season with fine salt and pepper and gratedginger, if youlike.

Spicy Veggie Broth
Serves 2

½ cup onion, chopped up nice and fine

1 tablespoon organically-sourced olive oil, optional

2 garlic cloves, skins removed and crushed

1 celery rib, sliced up nice and fine

½ bell pepper, chopped

1 teaspoon curry powder

1½ cups homemade veggie stock

½ cup broccoli

½ large cucumber, chopped up nice and fine

1 teaspoon vinegar that you like

Fine salt and pepper

¼ green herbs such as parsley, basil, or cilantro, sliced up coarsely

If you are using an electronic cooker or an Instant Pot: Set it to "Sauté".

If you have a manual cooker: Heat your stove plate to a medium-high heat.

Add the oil, if using. Add the onion, garlic, celery and bell pepper and cook for 2 to3 minutes, until they start to soften.

Add curry powder to taste and cook for 30 seconds.

Add in your stock.

Close the lid of your pot.

If you are using an electronic cooker or an Instant Pot: Put it on the manual setting and choose a low pressure. Set the time for 4 minutes and release the pressure quickly.

If you have a manual cooker: Heat your stove plate to a medium-high heat and allow the pressure to build up until it is low. Then cook for 4 minutes. And allow the pressure to be quickly released

Take the lid off with care in case there is any steam left.

Add the broccoli and cucumber.

Close the lid of your pot.

If you are using an electronic cooker or an Instant Pot: Put it on the manual setting and choose a high pressure. Set the time for 1minute and release the pressure quickly.

If you have a manual cooker: Heat your stove plate to a medium-high heat and allow the pressure to build up until it is high. Then cook for 1 minutes. And allow the pressure to be quickly released

Take the lid off with care in case there is any steam left.

Blend the soup carefully in a high-speed blender for the creamiest result, adding the herbs and vinegar while you blend.

Add fine salt and pepper to taste.

Chill soup overnight.

When ready to serve, taste the soup and adjust seasonings. Serve, garnished with diced avocado and colored peppers, if using.

Conclusion

Well, that's about all for the moment.

I really hope that you find these recipes inspiring and are ready to go and try them out for yourself.

Vegan cooking does not have to mean eating bland, boring food and, once you have tried some of the recipes in this book, your taste buds will thank you.

One last thing – would you please leave me a review on Amazon? I'd really like to know if you did love the book.

Click here to leave a review for this book on Amazon!

Thank you and good luck!

CHECK OUT MY OTHER BOOKS!!!

Visit Maria Hopkins on Amazon.com

55915122R00095

Made in the USA
Middletown, DE
12 December 2017